HUMOROUS STORIES: SQUEAKY CLEAN

An Indexed Collection of Humor

D. Bruce Barnes

D. BRUCE BARNES

D&B Publishing
Virginia Beach • Virginia

Copyright © 1999 by D. Bruce Barnes

All rights reserved. No part of this book may be reproduced for sale in any manner whatsoever without written permission, except in the case of brief quotations embodied in critical articles and reviews.

D&B Publishing
Virginia Beach, VA

Printed in the United States

With sincere love and appreciation, I dedicate this book to my mother and father, Donald and Irene Barnes. They helped my brother and me grow up with laughter and funny moments. They had the ability to help us keep a healthy outlook on life through the ridiculous. For this, I am glad!

Table of Contents

1. A Time for Speaking, A Time for Silence
2. Absent-Minded
3. All in Favor, Stand
4. Amazing Recovery
5. Annoyance, Anger, or Exasperation
6. Answer to Prayer
7. As You Would be Judged
8. Behold, I Come Quickly
9. Believing
10. Best Christmas Gift
11. Better Poverty
12. Better Solution
13. Big Imagination
14. Blue-Plate Special
15. Brave Fighter
16. Breakfast in Bed
17. Bury the Dead
18. But He Did
19. Cain's Wife
20. Calm and Serene?
21. Camp Food
22. Choir Refrain
23. Complaints
24. Continued State of Affairs
25. Correct Grammar
26. Counting on Luck
27. Curse of the Same Condition
28. Daisy's Advice
29. Dearly Beloved
30. Devil Made Me Do It
31. Dictator's Image
32. Directions to Heaven
33. Divine Help
34. Divine Will
35. Dog Funeral
36. Dust to Dust
37. Eating Before Preaching
38. Eenie, Meenie Minie, Moe
39. Expressions of Love?
40. Expressions of Satisfaction
41. Eye of the Beholder
42. Fair Fight?
43. Fairness
44. Financial Strain
45. Finding the Right Church
46. Fishy Methods
47. Fitting Text
48. Following an Example
49. Following Doctor's Orders
50. Fool's Name
51. Forgetfulness
52. Fortune, Misfortune
53. For What Ails You
54. Fourth Person
55. From the Floor
56. Frugal Strength
57. Gentleness
58. Getting on My Nerves
59. Getting What You Want
60. Ghostly Image
61. Going Nowhere Fast
62. Going Out
63. Good Deeds
64. Good Old Age
65. Good Witness
66. Grace Before Meals
67. Grandpa's Religion
68. Happy Ending
69. Hastiness
70. Haystack
71. He Won't Bite
72. Hearing What You Want
73. Henpecked
74. Hereafter
75. Herod's Answer
76. Holes in the Head
77. Hopeful Proposals
78. How to Get a Crowd
79. I Knew It
80. Ill-Informed

81.	Illiterate	127.	Not at Fault
82.	Imitation	128.	Not Good Enough
83.	Impossible Invention	129.	No so Bad After All
84.	In a Manner of Speaking	130.	Not What it Seems
85.	In Control		
86.	In the Middle	131.	Obituaries
87.	Indian Appraisal	132.	Offerings and Sacrifice
88.	Innovation	133.	Oh Susie!
89.	Insomnia	134.	Old Bore
90.	Intense Desire	135.	Old-Fashioned Discipline
91.	I've Had Enough	136.	Old Man, New Man
		137.	One for Me, One for God
92.	Job Qualifications	138.	Only Thirty-Two Days
93.	Just a Matter of Time	139.	Opportunity for a Witness
		140.	Optimism or Pessimism?
94.	Keep Feeding Her		
95.	Keeping Silence	141.	Pastoral Call
96.	Keeping Your Word	142.	Patience
97.	Knowing What to Say	143.	Persistence
98.	Knowing Your Place	144.	Perspective
		145.	Perverse Parakeet
99.	Late and In a Hurry	146.	Pig Toes
100.	Learning Politeness	147.	Piggish Behavior
101.	Listening to What You're Told	148.	Politeness
102.	Logic Problem	149.	Plenty for Everyone
103.	Looking Back	150.	Practice Makes Perfect
104.	Lord Knows	151.	Praise the Lord
105.	Lot to be Thankful For	152.	Preacher's Notes
106.	Love for Children	153.	Preparation for Life
107.	Lying	154.	Preparation for the After-Life
		155.	Prideful Approach
108.	Man in Charge	156.	Profanity
109.	Man or a Mouse?	157.	Profiting from Evil
110.	Many Marriages	158.	Promise of Better
111.	Marital Paradise	159.	Proper Protocol
112.	Matter of Perspective	160.	Protesting
113.	Mellow Voice	161.	Prunes
114.	Memorization		
115.	Memory Verse Overload	162.	Repetition
116.	Merely for Others to See	163.	Respect is in the Eye of the Beholder
117.	Mistaken Purpose		
118.	Money for College	164.	Right Answer
119.	Musical Taste	165.	Right Change
		166.	Righteous Indignation
120.	Name Calling	167.	Rmmmbumbum
121.	Near Impossible	168.	Rudolph
122.	Needing Help		
123.	Needing Rescue	169.	Seeking a Sign
124.	Newlywed Blues	170.	Self-Control
125.	Nightmare	171.	Sermon Assessment
126.	No Enemies	172.	Shorter Sermon 1

173. Shorter Sermon 2
174. Sermon Sleeping
175. Sin of Pride
176. Sin Will Find You Out
177. Sorry You're Gone
178. Speaker of Rank
179. Special Delivery
180. Spiritual Excitement
181. Standing in the Need of Prayer
182. Success Oriented
183. Successful Marriage
184. Surprise Visit
185. Swallow Hard
186. Swiping Swill

187. Tabloid Headlines
188. Take Him at His Word
189. Telemarketing
190. Telling the Truth
191. Terminal Case
192. Thankful for What You Get
193. That's What It Says
194. Told You
195. Tongue Tied
196. Too Many Questions
197. Truth or Pride
198. Turn it Off
199. Two-Faced

200. Ugly
201. Unpaid Debts
202. Untasty Diet Food
203. Updated Colloquialisms
204. Useless

205. Value of Education
206. Value of One's Spouse

207. Whatever You Think
208. What's in a Name
209. When You Grow Up
210. Which is Better?
211. Which Sermon?
212. Which Would You Rather Have?
213. Who's Crazy?
214. Who's King?
215. Working Day and Night
216. Worried About Nothing
217. Wrong Destination

218. "X" Marks the Spot

219. You First
220. You'd Never Believe It

221. Zaccheeus, Come Down

A

1. A Time for Speaking, A Time for Silence

Homer, a young country farm hand, was court'n his favorite girl from the back woods. On one particular night, they sat on the front porch swing of the old farm house; the moon was bright, and the stars twinkled in the distant darkness. The romance of the evening was strong, far too strong for Homer. He looked at his girl in the emotion of the moment and said, "Millie, wood'ja be . . . ya know, my wife?"

Of course, Millie was thrilled and accepted immediately, but there was dead silence from Homer for over thirty minutes. All that could be heard were the crickets, an occasional frog croaking along the river bank, and the slow squeak of the porch swing. Millie, not being able to stand the silence any longer, finally commented, "Homer? You're sayin' nary a thing." "Oh, Millie," Homer replied quite soberly, "I think I've said too much already!"

✦✦✦✦✦✦

2. Absent-Minded

An absent-minded professor was getting ready for his day of college teaching when his wife came and reminded him, "Honey, please remember that we are moving today. If you come back to this house after work, it will be empty."

The professor went about his day, but as usual, he forgot all about it. When he arrived and saw that the house was vacant, he recalled something about moving but mumbled to himself, "Now, where was it that we were moving to?"

He stood there on the sidewalk for a few moments thinking this over when he noticed a little girl playing in front of the house. He went over to the little girl and asked, "Little girl, pardon me. Did you see a moving van here at this house today?"

"Yes sir," she replied.

"Oh good!" said the professor, "Could you tell me which direction it went when it left?"

The little girl looked up, took him by the hand, and said, "Sure, Daddy, I'll show you."

✦✦✦✦✦✦

3. All in Favor, Stand

The pastor had become quite disturbed that the chairman of his deacon board always slept through his messages. He had talked to him about the situation, but no progress was ever made. The pastor was so upset, he finally decided to teach the old deacon a lesson.

During the middle of his Sunday sermon, while the deacon was sleeping soundly, the pastor announced very calmly and in a normal voice, "Everyone who wants to go to heaven, please stand." Everyone in the congregation stood—except the old deacon, of course. Once the pastor requested that the congregation be seated, he said, "Now, everyone who wants to go to hell . . ." and then the pastor yelled out, "please stand!"

Immediately, the old deacon bounded to his feet. He looked around in a daze, for a moment surveying what was going on. Still a little puzzled about the situation, he turned to the pastor and said, "Preacher, I don't know just what we're voting on, but it sure seems that you and I are the only ones in favor of doing it!"

❖❖❖❖❖❖

4. Amazing Recovery

A man and his wife were traveling down a country road when suddenly a rabbit ran out in front of the car, and with all attempts to avoid the little creature, they still ran over it. Stopping the car, they both rushed to the perishing animal. With one look, the lady ran back to the car, got an aerosol can, and came back to the dead rabbit. She sprayed him completely, and after just a few moments, the animal began to move its ears and then its legs. Amazingly enough, it sat up on the ground. It happily began to hop back to the woods, but about twenty feet away, it turned back to the couple and waved. It hopped another twenty feet, turned, and waved—and so it did until it disappeared into the woods.

The husband took the can from his wife and looked at the label. It said, "Hair (Hare) Restorer: Guaranteed to Create a Permanent Wave."

❖❖❖❖❖❖

5. Annoyance, Anger, or Exasperation

A young boy was studying his vocabulary words for school, but he had an especially difficult time understanding the variant meanings of "annoyance," "anger," and "exasperation." He went to his father and asked for help.

"Of course," replied the father, "it is simply a difference in degrees. Let me illustrate it for you. Pick up the phone extension in the hallway, and listen to what happens." The lad did so, and the father dialed a number at random, someone he nor the family knew. Once the party answered the phone, the father said, "Hello! I would like to speak to Jack, please." The answer came back, "There is no one here named Jack. Would you please carefully look up the proper number before you call people on the phone?" With that, all parties hung up. The father looked at the son and said, "See son, this man's reaction on the phone was 'annoyance.'"

"Now, pick up the phone again and listen to what happens." The father once again calls the same number. The other party picks up the phone, and the father says, "Hello! I would like to speak to Jack, please." The answer came back a little stronger this time, "What? Didn't I just tell you that there is no Jack here. I don't know what is wrong with people like you who have no more sense not to check out the numbers you call. Don't call this number again!" The man slammed the phone receiver down, and the father looked at his son and said, "Now this time, this man showed us the meaning of 'anger.'"

"Okay, let's get on the phone once more, and I will show you what the word 'exasperation' means." The father once again calls the same number. The same man answers the call when the father says, "Hello! This is Jack. Have there been any calls for me?"

◆◆◆◆◆◆

6. **Answer to Prayer**

A little girl went and told her mother how cruel to animals a little neighborhood boy was. She explained how the boy had set various snares and traps for the innocent fowls. She went on to tell her mother how she had sincerely prayed about the situation.

"First, Momma, I prayed that the mean boy would change his mind and heart about doing this; but he didn't, because he set the traps anyway. Next, I prayed that God would not let the little birds go in the traps, but they did anyway. Then I prayed that the snares would not work, but they did work, and rather well at that."

"Well, dear," replied Momma, "You did all that you could."

"No, Momma, that's not all! God answered my last prayer. I asked the Lord to make me strong and courageous."

"And He answered that prayer?"

"Yes, Momma, 'cause I went around and smashed all of those traps to pieces with a hammer!"

7. As You Would Be Judged

In a less civilized nation than our own, an old man in the family had grown weak, frail, and unable to work. Because he was eating too much food for his supposed usefulness to the family, his eldest son loaded the aged gentleman into a wheelbarrow and began to cart him to a high mountain. The plan was to leave him there and let him die. Also, the eldest son took along his oldest son, about eight years old, to explain why this was necessary.

"Son," he said, "your grandfather is old and useless to everyone. All he does is eat and take from the rest of us that which would make life easier for those of us who are young. We will place him high on this mountain, and there, leave him to die. This will be best for everyone."

The little boy responded, "Father, I am glad you have explained this to me and that you have taken me along to see this done. Now, I will know what to do with you when you are old."

✦✦✦✦✦✦

B

8. Behold, I Come Quickly

A young preacher just out of seminary had been taught that the best preaching would be without notes and from memory. He had practiced his message, and he felt ready for his first Sunday message. He came to the pulpit and announced his text for the morning saying, "I will be preaching this morning from Revelation 22:7, 'Behold, I come quickly.'" Suddenly, he realized that he could not remember what was to come next. So once again, repeating his text but this time with more emphasis and a pound of the pulpit, he spoke out, "My text for this service is, 'Behold I come quickly.'" Still, he came to an immediate halt. A little embarrassed but still determined, he started from the beginning increasing his volume even more and striking the pulpit several times, "My text for the sermon today is, 'Behold, I come quickly."

With his excitement, he accidently pushed forward too much on the pulpit. It fell from the platform tossing the young preacher over it onto the lap of a young lady seated on the front row. After what seemed like irrecoverable embarrassment, the young preacher once again returned to the platform where he straightway began an apology to the young lady saying, "I sincerely express my apology to the young lady on the front row for this terrible accident."

"Oh, don't worry about that," she said, "I should have been prepared. You told me three times that you were coming!"

✦✦✦✦✦✦

9. Believing

In a Christian day care, a teacher was giving a kindergarten class time for "sharing." The children became more and more relaxed with sharing their feelings as each spoke. The special topic of the day concerned what they believed in. The teacher was especially interested in using the discussion to introduce the subject of belief and faith in the Lord. As the "sharing" ensued among the youngsters, the teacher was pleased that the children themselves had turned the dialogue to that very topic. As the sharing time was going around the circle, one child said, "I believe in the Lord."

"I believe in Jesus, too," said the next.

When it came Janie's time, she said, "I believe in everything!"

"What do you mean by that?" asked another child.

"Well," said Janie, "Jesus, Moses, Santa, Snow White, the Tooth Fairy, you know, I believe in everything!"

❖❖❖❖❖❖

10. Best Christmas Gift

The parents of an especially rambunctious young boy were debating about what to get him for Christmas. Many items were discussed that were both practical as well as frivolous. As they discussed different possibilities, they always seemed to consider how each gift would affect his character and if they could stand to be close to the active primary while he was playing with the toy. Finally they began to seriously discuss one special gift.

"I think we should get him a new bicycle for Christmas," said Mother.

"Perhaps," said Father, "but, do you think a bicycle would significantly change his behavior?"

"I don't think so," said the mother, "but at least it will spread it more consistently over a wider area!"

❖❖❖❖❖❖

11. Better Poverty

A local town drunk went to a revival meeting and was wonderfully saved. With his entire life changed, he testified of the Lord everywhere he went. Attempting to be faithful in every area of his life, he went to a Sunday service and placed the last dollar he had in the offering plate; because he had no money, he had to walk home. On his way home, he met on a street corner the bartender who used to serve him alcohol. The bartender, discovering why the former alcoholic was walking home, began to ridicule the man for giving his last money to the church. He said, "You are indeed a foolish man. You give your last dollar to the church and then have to walk home."

The unwavering young Christian retorted, "Yes, but I am not half the fool I used to be when I would give you my last dollar and not be able to walk home!"

❖❖❖❖❖❖

12   Better Solution

Patient: (speaking to a psychiatrist) Doc, you've got to help me; my life is in turmoil, and I am hardly getting any sleep. As I lay on my bed at night, I keep imagining that someone's under the bed. I try to deal with it as long as I can, but fear gets the better of me, so I lie down on the floor so I can see under the bed. I lie there for a little while; then, I begin to fear that someone is on top of the bed. Yet, when I get back on the bed, I again fear what's under the bed. Doc, all night long I'm up and down and up and down. I just don't believe I can stand it any longer.

Psychiatrist: Yes, your case appears quite serious, but I do believe I can help you. In order to do so, I need to see you twice a week for the next two years. My fee per hour is $100; however, I am confident I can cure your of these fears.

Patient: Doc, that would be great, but that's a lot of money. I'll have to talk it over with my wife. I'll let you know our decision next week.

As agreed, the man called the psychiatrist the next week.

Patient: Doc, I won't need your services after all. When my wife heard how much this was going to cost, she cured my problem.
Psychiatrist: Really? How so?
Patient: She cut the legs off the bed!

✦✦✦✦✦✦

13.   Big Imagination

A man was visiting an insane asylum, and he was allowed to freely walk through the hallways observing the people housed there. One particular man caught his eye, for he was walking very slowly. The visitor stepped up to the man and noticed that his hands were cupped together as if he were hiding something.

Visitor: Excuse me. You have caught my interest. What are you holding in your hands?
Inmate: Just try to guess.
Visitor: A thousand dollars?
Inmate: (Peeked in his hands): Nope! Try again.
Visitor: A limousine?
Inmate: (Peeked in his hands): Nope! Try again.

Visitor:	A yacht?
Inmate:	(Peeked in his hands): Nope! Try again.
Visitor:	A horse?
Inmate:	(Peeked in his hands and then peered sheepishly at the visitor): "What color?"

✦✦✦✦✦✦

14. Blue-Plate Special

A Navy recruit, a rather small man, had received his first shore leave. Not knowing anyone in the port where the ship had docked, he strolled through the town on a sight-seeing trip just to pass the time. While walking downtown, he happened upon a little café that offered a "blue-plate special" meal for a very reasonable price. He went inside to enjoy a quiet meal.

He approached the counter and sat on a stool next to one of the largest Marines he had ever seen. The Navy-man ordered his special and sat there quietly. Once the meal arrived, he noticed that it needed a little salt, so he tapped the Marine on the shoulder and politely requested that he pass the salt. With that, the Marine jumped from his stool, picked up the Navy man and began pounding him left and right, up and down. This went on for some time until the little Navy man lay on the floor in a heap. The huge Marine towering over him, looked down, and said, "Kick boxing: mastered it while stationed down under." The Marine went back to his stool and ordered another blue-plate special.

After a while the small Navy man got up, brushed himself off, and quietly returned to his meal by the Marine. The little man went on eating his meal without salt, but in a short while, he needed to wipe his mouth with a napkin, so he tapped the Marine on the shoulder and requested that he pass a napkin. Once again, the Marine began to throw the Navy man all over the café, against this wall and that, to the ceiling and several times to the floor. Just like before, the Navy man lay on the floor in a heap. The Marine stood over the little man and said, "Judo master: learned it while stationed in Japan." The Marine returned to his stool and ordered another blue-plate special.

Once the Navy man regained his ability to stand, he returned to his stool beside the Marine and continued eating his meal without salt or napkins. As the small man was nearly half finished, he noticed that the straws he needed for his milk were a little out of reach, so he tapped the Marine on the shoulder and requested a straw. The irritated Marine began chopping at the little man up, down, and all around. This went on for several minutes until the Navy man lay in the corner, a heap of mangled flesh and blood. The Marine stood over him and said, "Karate:

became a Black Belt while stationed in Korea." The Marine returned to his stool and ordered his fourth blue-plate special.

It took some time, but the Navy man finally got up, paid for his meal without a word, and left the café. About thirty minutes later, the Marine was on his fifth blue-plate special when the Navy man returned to the café. He went straight over to the Marine, tapped him on the shoulder, and as he turned, the Navy man began bashing on the Marine without mercy. The Marine was now the one bouncing from the walls and ceiling. After about five minutes of this, the Marine lay in the corner out cold, a heap of flesh and blood. The little Navy man spoke to the café owner behind the counter, "When this man wakes up, please tell him for me: 'Crowbar: bought it at Sears and Roebuck.'"

✦✦✦✦✦✦

15. Brave Fighter

A young lad of eight arrived home a little afraid to explain to Mother that he had been in a fight. There he stood like a little warrior (one who had obviously lost his battle) with his lip cut, eye blackened, nose bleeding, and clothes tattered.

"Oh, Johnny," said Mother, "You've been in another fight!"

"But Mother," whimpered Johnny, "I couldn't help it this time. I was trying to keep a little boy from being beaten up by a bigger boy."

"I'm so sorry, Johnny!" said Mother, "I'm glad that you were a responsible little man to stand up for that little boy. That was mighty brave. Who was the little boy?"

"Me, Mother."

✦✦✦✦✦✦

16. Breakfast in Bed

Sam and Anne were spending a lot of time together, and their relationship was getting quite serious. As with most young couples, they were not only getting to know each other better, they were learning more about their families—the in-laws. In fact, Anne was very impressed with Sam's parents and how much they showed their love for each other. "How thoughtful they are of one another," Anne said. "I can't express how impressed I am that your father brings your mother breakfast in bed every morning."

With the passing of time, Sam and Anne's relationship progressed to engagement and eventually marriage. Just after the beautiful wedding and the wonderful reception, they were on the way to their honeymoon. Still filled with the sense of wonder, Anne once again mentioned to Sam about how marvelous it was that his father would bring his mother breakfast in bed every morning. She went a little further this time. "Tell me," she questioned slowly and hopefully, "does it run in the family?"

"It definitely does, my dear," said Sam, "and I take after my mother!"

✦✦✦✦✦✦

17. Bury the Dead

In a small country town, the pastor came to the church early only to find that right in front of the church, a mule was dead in the street. By all appearances, the mule had been involved in an accident of some kind during the night Saturday. The pastor went to the church phone and called the town mayor about the animal.

The mayor was not pleased to have been awakened on his Sunday morning, and he retorted to the preacher, "Why are you calling me? I thought you preachers are supposed to bury the dead!"

"You're right, Mr. Mayor, we do," answered the pastor, "however, we are obligated to notify the next of kin first."

✦✦✦✦✦✦

18. But He Did

A man was a second-shift worker at the local factory, one which was not too far from his home. He had made it his practice to walk home after work; it helped him wind down a little as well as save some money on transportation. This method worked out well for him, and he discovered two routes he could take home. If not too tired, he would take the long way; however, if really exhausted, he would take the short cut. The only problem with the short cut was that it passed through a cemetery, and he did not like that way very much because it was a little scary in the middle of the night.

On one particular evening, he was quite tired. Reassuring his nerves, he decided to go through the graveyard. It was an unusually dark night, and unbeknownst to him, a new grave had been dug for an early morning burial. He walked along and straightway fell into the freshly dug grave.

He yelled and screamed for help, but no one heard. He attempted to climb or jump out but to no avail. After about thirty minutes of attempts, he gave up and decided to wait until morning when someone would come by and help him. He curled up at one end of the grave and went to sleep.

    A hour or so later, another man, one who was a little inebriated, was also walking through the cemetery. He, too, fell into the grave. Just as the factory worker, he tried to climb and jump out, but he was unsuccessful. As he began to yell and scream, he woke up the man who had been sleeping at the other end of the grave.

    The factory worker spoke up boldly, "You can't get out of here!"

    But, he did!

✦✦✦✦✦✦

C

19. Cain's Wife

A preacher had spent a great deal of time talking with a man concerning his need of faith and about the Lord. It certainly appeared that progress was being made until the man, in trying to change the subject, used a familiar tactic of diversion. He said, "Preacher, all of this may be important, but what I want to know is, where did Cain get his wife?"

The preacher determined not to be led off track replied, "I truly am moved by those who seek to have more knowledge; however, I must warn you of the danger of losing sight of salvation, as many have before, when they begin to think and inquire about another man's wife."

✦✦✦✦✦✦

20. Calm and Serene?

A well-known pastor had always appeared in control of his manners and ministry. People spoke well of him in relation to this because his demeanor always seemed poised; yet, he accomplished more than the usual pastor.

He was once speaking to his congregation about this perception that everyone had of him, and he said, "In this matter, I am very much like a swan." He continued to explain, "You see, I look all calm and serene on the surface, but underneath, I'm paddling like crazy!"

✦✦✦✦✦✦

21. Camp Food

The teen week at church camp was a great experience for the campers. Through the services, many lives were changed: some for conversion, some for dedication, and some for Christian service. The teens took for their theme the song, "Where He Leads Me, I Will Follow." They sang it practically everywhere they went around camp.

On their last day of camp, the teens came to the mess hall for their last meal together before going home. To their surprise, the camp cook served up leftovers from the week. Many of the teens began grumbling and complaining about the food.

The murmuring became so widespread that the camp director heard it. He stood and announced to the group, "If you are going to complain about the food, I really think you should keep this in mind. Please don't sing 'Where He Leads Me, I Will Follow' until you are willing to say, 'What He feeds me, I will swallow!'"

✦✦✦✦✦✦

22. Choir Refrain

A spirited revival had been sweeping the mountainous community. The church was filled with many newcomers, and various people were converted including some of the community moonshiners. The Sunday following the revival's conclusion, the pastor stood on Sunday morning and announced the grand results the meeting had in so many lives. Just before the choir sang its benedictory refrain at the close of the service, the pastor remarked in his closing prayer,

"Dear Lord, you did a great work among these people this week. We see here in our services many who were changed because of this revival meeting. In fact, Lord, some here were moonshiners, until you changed 'em. And Lord, I thank you that these men took their liquor stills and broke 'em up—broke 'em up indeed, and thank you Lord, that they poured all that illegal and evil elixir into the river. Amen."

While the pastor walked down the aisle greeting the church goers, everyone's attention was arrested as the choir began to sing their benediction refrain, "Let Us Gather at the River."

✦✦✦✦✦✦

23. Complaints

Three young men came to a monastery where all the monks take a vow of silence. According to the head of the abbey, each one would be able to speak one short sentence on alternating years. The time passed and at breakfast, the first monk received his moment to speak. Looking over his breakfast bowl, he said, "I hate oatmeal." Everyone continued on as before. Another year passed, and the time arrived for the second monk to utter his brief comment. At the breakfast table, he remarked, "I like oatmeal." Everyone continued on in silence. At the completion of the third year, the third monk came down to the breakfast table with suitcase in hand. As his moment to speak came, he rebuked, "All you guys do is complain about oatmeal. I'm leaving!"

✦✦✦✦✦✦

24. Continued State of Affairs

An Assyrian inscription which was carved in stone tablets about 1500 B.C. reportedly described the following state of affairs: "The earth is depraved in these last days; many signs indicate that the world is coming to a speedy end; bribery and corruption are commonplace; children fail to obey their parents; all men want to write books; the end of the world is near."

◆◆◆◆◆◆

25. Correct Grammar

The mother and father of an independently thinking little boy were both professors of English at the nearby college. Attempting to train their little neophyte early in life in all the finer ways of grammar, they had been recently emphasizing how important it was that he not end sentences with prepositions. The little boy understood more than the parents gave him credit for, but being a somewhat resourceful child, he was quite tired of the persistent grammar lessons at home. As he was getting ready for bed upstairs, his mother got a book from their library on the finer points of English grammar. She was going to read to him from this tedious volume, after she tucked him in bed, rather than from an interesting story book which he really wanted. Standing at the top of the stairs with his little PJ's on and seeing his mother coming to the stairs with the thick grammar book in tow, he said forthrightly, "Now Mother, what are you bringing that book I don't want to be read to out of up for?"

◆◆◆◆◆◆

26. Counting on Luck

Jason: I really thought that today was my lucky day.
Jeremy: How so?
Jason: Well, I awoke this morning at 7:00 o'clock on this seventh day of the seventh month. I made seven successful sales calls and received seven commission bonuses. I had lunch with seven friends, and my bill came to exactly seven dollars. I had seven dollars in my pocket when I drove by a horse race. There were seven races and seven horses in the seventh race. So, I bet my seven dollars on the seventh horse at exactly 7:00 o'clock in the evening.

Jeremy: Wow! And your horse won?
Jason: No. Unfortunately, he came in seventh.

✦✦✦✦✦✦

27. Curse of the Same Condition

A mother was telling a friend about her son and her daughter. Both siblings were married, and the mother was explaining how each was faring in their respective marriages. She went on to tell her friend, "Oh, my daughter has a wonderful marriage! She married a remarkable young man who is so considerate and always helps her around the house. He will wash the dishes, help clean up the house, take care of the baby, and even cooks many of their meals. My daughter is so blessed."

"But, oh, my son! His marriage is not a good one at all; in fact, the woman he married is so dominating. Do you know that she expects him to wash the dishes, help clean up the house, take care of the baby, and even cook many of their meals. My son has it so hard. I really feel sorry for him!"

✦✦✦✦✦✦

D

28. Daisy's Advice

A man was driving through the country when his car stalled. He got out and opened the hood to see what the problem might be. He had looked at several things when a cow came alongside the car and looked under the hood also. After a moment, the cow said, "The trouble is in your carburetor."

The driver was so shocked at hearing the cow speak that he ran down the road until he came to the first farm house. He told the farmer all that had happened. The farmer asked, "Was that cow white with black spots, and did she have a diamond-shaped spot between her eyes?" "Yes," the man replied.

"Oh, don't listen to her," the farmer retorted, "Daisy knows nothing about cars!"

✦✦✦✦✦✦

29. Dearly Beloved

Four widows were talking about their churches and the problems each congregation was facing in attendance. The longer the conversation went, the more each lady attempted to "outdo" the others in defining just how bad things had gotten in attendance.

Widow 1: We're a large congregation, but we lose over half of our Sunday morning attendance for the Sunday evening service.
Widow 2: At my church, we lose so many for our Sunday night service that we only have about thirty show up.
Widow 3: That's nothing at all! Sometimes our evening service will be down to about 10.
Widow 4: Well, it's so bad at our church on Sunday night that when the pastor says, "Dearly beloved," it makes me think that he's proposing!

✦✦✦✦✦✦

30. Devil Made Me Do It

A young boy, Mike, wanted to go down to the river and play with his friends in the water. His mother refused the request because there would be no parental supervision. He protested vigorously, but his mother began talking to him about obedience to parents, about obeying the Lord, and about denying the will of the devil in his young life. The advice his mother had given him came from several portions of the Scripture such as "Resist the devil, and he will flee from you," and the place where Jesus said, "Get thee behind me, Satan." He took the Scriptural admonitions seriously and promised to put them into practice. About an hour later, Mike came home but was drenched from head to toe.

Mother: Mike! You have disobeyed me and went swimming in the river anyway!

Mike: But Mother, I didn't mean for this to happen. I didn't mean to do wrong.

Mother: Didn't I tell you that if the devil tempted you to tell him to get behind you?

Mike: And that's just what I did. I was standing on the river bank wanting to jump in, but I told the devil to get behind me. And no sooner did he get back there than that old rascal just pushed me right in!

❖❖❖❖❖❖

31. Dictator's Image

The dictator of a small country was pleased to see his image and likeness observable anywhere in the country. He was especially thrilled about the nation's postmaster producing a letter stamp with his picture on it. The dictator thought how wonderful to have his effigy in every home in the country as well as intersecting every road and passageway. After the stamp was in production, the dictator was greatly displeased that it was not selling very well. He summoned the nation's postmaster to find out the reason why. The postmaster said, "People are complaining that the stamps do not stick!"

The dictator snatched one from the postmaster, licked it, and stuck it on an envelope. "Look at that!" he screamed. "It sticks flawlessly!"

"Uh-oh," the postmaster responded hesitantly, "I see what the problem is now, sir. People have been spitting on the wrong side."

❖❖❖❖❖❖

Humorous Stories

32. Directions to Heaven

A famous evangelist, in an unfamiliar town for a revival, asked a local boy how to get to the post office. "Down two blocks, then one to the left," the boy replied.

"Thank you," said the evangelist. "Do you know who I am?" "Nope."

"I'm a famous preacher. If you come and hear me tonight, I'll show you the way to get to heaven." "Oh, go on," said the little boy. "You don't even know the way to the post office."

❖❖❖❖❖❖

33. Divine Help

A church youth group was needing to raise some funds to help with a summer mission's trip. In order for everyone in the group to get the needed money, the youth pastor decided to pull everyone together for a car wash. The proper promotion was done within the congregation as well as in the community. When the day arrived for the car wash, all the teenagers arrived at the proper place for the event. The only problem was that a big rain storm had moved into the area, and this threatened to dissolve the hope of any profits. The day promised to be a disaster until one teenager had a brainstorm. She came out with a new poster to hold next to the road as cars passed by. It read, "We Wash! God Rinses!" Business boomed.

❖❖❖❖❖❖

34. Divine Will

The pastor and his family went to see a local football game, and the youngest son noticed that the teams paused for prayer before beginning the game. The boy asked his father, "Dad, I was just wondering something. If both teams pray requesting divine help, and each of the prayers are equally acceptable to God, who would win the game?"

"Well, son," replied the pastor, "in a case like that, I believe even the Lord Himself would take the time to sit back and watch one fine football game."

❖❖❖❖❖❖

35. Dog Funeral

A man had a dog that was his pride and joy. Unfortunately, the dog died.

Wanting to do something special for his dear departed companion, the man came to the local Baptist pastor to ask for help. He knocked on the door, and when the pastor arrived there, the man asked, "Pastor, my dog died, and I want to know if you will help me make funeral arrangements and if you will preach a funeral service for him."

Pastor: Well, really, I'm sorry (wanting to avoid the thought altogether). My schedule is just so busy at this time, there is just no way that I could do it. You might try the Methodist preacher down the road; he could probably do it.
Stranger: I do appreciate the suggestion. Do you believe I should give that preacher remuneration for his services?
Pastor: Yes, it is always appropriate to do something of that nature for the service rendered.
Stranger: Well, Pastor, do you think $5,000 would be too little to give him?
Pastor: What? Wait a minute. You never told me that he was a Baptist dog!

❖❖❖❖❖❖

36. Dust to Dust

A little boy who just returned home from church had a question for his mother. "Mother, is it true that we're made of dust?"

"Yes, dear. That's true."

"And do we go back to dust when we die?" he asked.

"Yes, dear. The Bible teaches that also. Why do you ask?"

"Well, Mother, last night when I was kneeling by my bed to say my prayers, I looked under the bed, and I found someone who was either coming or going!"

❖❖❖❖❖❖

E

37. Eating Before Preaching

An evangelist was beginning a revival meeting in an old country church, and he was being housed for the week by one of the farming families of the church. The wife prepared a good meal for the family and the evangelist, and she called for everyone to come to the table. The evangelist kindly said, "I do appreciate the meal, but I will need to wait until after the service to eat. I just don't preach very good at all if I eat before preaching." With that, the evangelist went to his room and waited for the service time to arrive.

Well, the farmer was a little bothered by the evangelist's refusal to eat, so he decided he would stay home from the service. When the family returned that evening after the service, the farmer asked his wife, "How was the sermon?" She replied, "He should have gone ahead and ate supper!"

✦✦✦✦✦✦

38. Eenie, Meenie, Minie, Moe

A husband and wife were especially impressed by the expression, "Eenie, meenie, minie, moe." Although this seemed very unusual to everyone who knew them, this couple used the expression as inspiration for the naming of their children.

The first child born to their home, they named "Eenie."

The second-born, they named, "Meenie."

The third one they called "Minie."

However, when the fourth was born, they named him, "Homer."

A friend was quite puzzled by the change from the pattern he had seen developing, and he hoped for a plausible explanation. Finally, he got up enough nerve to ask the parents why they digressed from the original "Eenie, meenie, minie, moe." They replied, "Oh, that's easy to explain. We simply don't want any 'moe.'"

✦✦✦✦✦✦

39. Expressions of Love?

An older couple in the church always appeared to be so much in love. They had smiles on their faces whenever they were together, and they quietly laughed with each other as they spoke privately. The pastor had even noticed how much in love they were, for all during the service—every service—they would hold hands.

One Sunday after the morning service, the pastor felt compelled to tell the couple of his respect. He said, "I consider it quite inspirational to all the other couples, especially the younger ones, that you still express your love for each other after all these years. I am especially fond of seeing you hold hands during the services."

The wife spoke out quickly, "It's not love, Preacher. I'm just trying to keep the old coot from cracking his knuckles!"

✦✦✦✦✦✦

40. Expressions of Satisfaction

A lady was going on her very first bus trip across the state. She was quite nervous but also more than a little irritating to the driver and other passengers with her endless comments and questions. After several hours of non-stop talk right behind the driver's ear, she asked the driver, "How do you know where my stop is and how will I know where my stop is and when will I know it's time to get off the bus and...." The driver interrupted her as he looked in the mirror above his head, "Lady, you'll know it when you see the big smile on my face!"

✦✦✦✦✦✦

41. Eye of the Beholder

Two men, one an optimist and the other a pessimist, were employed by a shoe company to be door-to-door salesmen. Each was assigned a new territory where no salesmen had been before, two isolated islands in the Pacific Ocean. The following telegrams were sent to the home office one week after they arrived at their destinations.

Pessimist: Returning home. No one wears shoes here. No market.
Optimist: No one wears shoes here. Wide-open market. Send more salesmen!

✦✦✦✦✦✦

F

42. Fair Fight?

Little Jeremy came home from school the picture of one who had lost a recent fight. His clothes were torn from head to toe, and he had scratch marks on his face as well as a bloody nose. While his Dad was bandaging up Jeremy's wounds, he asked what had happened.

"Dad," said Little Jeremy, "I got tired of the neighborhood bully pushing everyone around. So, I tried to be a noble knight and challenge him to a duel. And just to make it fair, I gave him his choice of weapons."

"Well, Jeremy," said Dad, "that does seem like a noble and fair thing to do."
"Yes sir, it was. But there was only one problem. I never imagined he'd choose his big brother!"

✦✦✦✦✦✦

43. Fairness

Two men, always great rivals with each other, came to the first hole of the golf course. The first man teed up his ball and hit a magnificent drive. The ball hit on the green and lazily dropped in the cup. The second man teed up his ball and said, "Now after I hit my practice shot too, we'll begin our game."

✦✦✦✦✦✦

44. Financial Strain

Ray was in the throes of a financial crisis when he received an unexpected bill for $367, due within fifteen days. In complete frustration and disgust, he penned the following letter.

Dear Sirs:

>I am making a reply to your recent letter showing that I owe you $367.00. Quite frankly, I was not expecting this bill so soon, much less the short period of time you have given me to pay it. I want to meet my financial responsibilities, but I must tell you of my situation.

At present, I am having to maintain car insurance, home owner's insurance, mortgage insurance, life insurance, liability insurance, theft insurance, flood insurance, fire insurance, accidental death insurance all from which there is no complete assurance.

Additionally, I am expected to purchase a driver's license, car license, business license, hunting license, fishing license, motorcycle license, marriage license, and dog license. If this were not enough, I am forced to pay income tax, sales tax, business tax, school tax, gas tax, food tax, social security tax, excise tax, import tax, and floor tacks—each making me feel that I am being attacked!

As I go about personal business, I am constantly suspected, inspected, expected, but never respected. I am also pressed to give to every charitable organization such as world relief, child relief, homeless relief, minority relief, women's relief, and hunger relief. My money is requested of the Red Cross, but more of it goes to the double cross.

My financial status has been bleak due to federal laws, state laws, county laws, city laws, tax laws, mother-in-laws, sister-in-laws, outlaws, and cole slaw. But I made up a batch of slaw and sold it so I could get you your enclosed money.

Sincerely,
Ray

✦✦✦✦✦✦

45. Finding the Right Church

A man had been skipping from church to church, trying to find just the right one: a church that was friendly and one that had people like him. He slipped in late to one church across town at the time the pastor was reading his sermon text from Romans 7:18-19, "... how to perform that which is good I find not. For the good that I would I do not: but the evil which I would not, that I do."

As the man sat on the pew, he sighed with relief, "Thank goodness! I've finally found a group of people just like me!"

✦✦✦✦✦✦

46. Fishy Methods

A man in the community had gotten a reputation for always catching his quota of fish wherever he went, but no one knew how he did it. His effectiveness had become so much the topic of discussion, that it finally came to the ears of the game warden. On one fishing trip, the game warden secretly followed him. After the man had put his boat into the water and traveled to a secluded spot on the lake, the man anchored his line and began making his preparation for fishing.

The game warden pulled his boat up next to the man, told him who he was, and that he had come to fish beside him that day. The man told him that would be fine, and with that, the man lit a stick of dynamite and threw it in the water. The TNT exploded and fish began to float to the top.

The game warden went ballistic himself. He yelled at the man, "You can't do that! That's against the law!"

The man lit another stick of dynamite and threw it on the game warden's lap saying, "Look, are you gonna' talk or fish?"

✦✦✦✦✦✦

47. Fitting Text

A revivalist was called to preach a series special evangelistic services at a local church, but the man's stature was more than on the small side. As he arose to the rather large podium, the congregation could hardly see the man's head over the pulpit. He announced, "My text for tonight is found in Matthew 14:27, 'Be not afraid; it is I.'" The congregation could hardly contain itself from the humor of the situation, because his presence was less then intimidating. Although embarrassed a little from the circumstance, he went on with his message.

In order to resolve the problem for the next night's meeting, several hymnals were placed behind the pulpit on which the evangelist could stand. As he got up to preach, he steadied himself on the books; however, as he began to open his Bible and introduce his text, the hymnals shifted under his weight toppling the little man flat on the floor. After again arranging the books for his platform, he was doubly embarrassed as he read his preselected text for the evening (John 16:16): "A little while, and ye shall not see me."

✦✦✦✦✦✦

48. Following an Example

A father had been having a difficult time getting his son to study and to excel in his academics, but nothing seemed to work. Finally, when the young man's report card came out with grades expressive of his lack of effort, the father sternly reported, "Son, how do you ever expect to amount to anything except you start applying yourself to your studies. Don't you realize that by your age, Abraham Lincoln was already studying to be a lawyer?"

"Dad, you're right," the boy admitted, "And from what I've learned in school, that by your age he was already President of the United States."

✦✦✦✦✦✦

49. Following Doctor's Orders

A husband and wife were having some marital difficulties—always fighting, arguing, and spouting off at each other—so the husband thought it best to get himself some counseling help. After the husband and marriage counselor met for some time, the counselor suggested a means of remedying the moments of friction between the couple. The counselor advised, "I propose that you run five miles each day for a week. This will not only help you health-wise, but it will most probably help you relieve some of the hostilities and frustrations you feel. Once you have completed this assignment, call me back in a week."

The husband agreed to follow the advice. A week later the counselor received the call from the husband as requested. "Well," said the counselor, "tell me how things are going between you and your wife?"

"How should I know?" said the husband. "As of today, I'm thirty-five miles away!"

✦✦✦✦✦✦

50. Fool's Name

During one of Dwight Moody's evangelistic campaigns, it was reported that just previous to one of the services, a man delivered a large envelope to him. Because the envelope looked important, he opened it to find one sheet of paper inside with only one word written on it—"FOOL."

He thought for a second and announced to the waiting crowd, "I have been given a special note here that has only one word on it, the word "fool." I must say that I have often gotten letters where someone has forgotten to sign his name. But never until now have I had someone who signed his name but forgot to write the letter!"

✦✦✦✦✦✦

51. Forgetfulness

There were three elderly ladies who were beginning to have increasing problems with their memories. As they sat together for mid-afternoon coffee and cake, one of them said, "You know, sometimes I get so confused. I find myself at the bottom of the stairs, and I can't remember whether I was coming down to get something or going up to put something away."

The second woman spoke of a similar experience saying, "The same type of thing happens to me. I will find myself standing at the refrigerator, and I can't remember whether I just put something in or whether I am there to get something out. It's so frustrating."

The third woman confidently said, "Well, I am glad that I don't have anything like that happen to me, at least not yet. But, I better knock on wood." She knocked on the table three times. No sooner had she finished, that she looked startled and said to her guests, "Excuse me, I think someone's at the door."

✦✦✦✦✦✦

52. Fortune, Misfortune

A man was working on a new high-rise building, and his job demanded that he lean far over the edge of the construction girders. While doing so . . .

Unfortunately, he slipped and fell over the girders.
Fortunately, he was only on the third story of the building.
Unfortunately, it was still high enough to kill him.
Fortunately, there was a hay wagon traveling slowly under the building.
Unfortunately, there was a pitchfork sticking prongs up in the hay.
Fortunately, he didn't fall on the pitchfork.
Unfortunately, he didn't fall on the hay wagon either.

✦✦✦✦✦✦

53. For What Ails You

A man was having grave physical problems that required him to follow the doctor's orders precisely. In preparation for this man's recovery to health, the doctor talked to the man's wife. He told her, "At all costs, your husband must have peace and quiet. He desperately needs his rest. I am giving you some sleeping pills. I'm sure that this will help him immensely."

"But how often should I give these to him?" she asked the doctor.

"Oh," said the physician, "I'm afraid you don't understand. The sleeping pills are for you!"

✦✦✦✦✦✦

54. Fourth Person

The most recent Sunday school lessons being studied by the children were about Jesus' early life and his family's flight into Egypt to escape the terror of Herod. In order to reinforce the lesson, the teacher asked the children to draw and color their idea of what it was like for Mary, Joseph, and Jesus to travel to this far away land.

As the teacher went from child to child seeing their pictures, she came to Jeremy who had drawn a picture of an airplane. Looking closely, she saw that there were four people in the plane.

She said to Jeremy, "That is surely an interesting picture. I see that you have Joseph, Mary, and that little one there must be Jesus. But who is the fourth person I see there at the front of the plane?"

"Oh," said Jeremy, "that's Pontius the pilot."

✦✦✦✦✦✦

55. From the Floor

A college professor, greatly loved but absent-minded, had made it his practice after covering a unit of class lectures, to dedicate one class period for student questions. He and the students enjoyed the special time of interaction with each other and the important information. The day for questions had arrived, but the absent-minded professor forgot to take his prescription medicine for an inner ear infection he was attempting to cure.

As he rose from his chair, the room began to spin round and round, and he staggering, immediately fell to the stage. In order to calm the concerned class, he said, "I think I'll postpone any personal comments and simply take questions from the floor!"

✦✦✦✦✦✦

56. Frugal Strength

A strongman at the circus sideshow enjoyed displaying his great feats of might. On one particular night, he had an unusually large audience, and he decided to end his performance with one of his favorite exhibitions. He took a lemon and squeezed the juice from it between his hands. After doing so, he made an offer to the crowd saying, "I will give $200 to any person in the audience who can squeeze even one more drop from this lemon."

Just then, a frail, scholarly-looking gentleman came to the center ring. He gripped the lemon, strained with all his little might, and squeezed out two drops. The strongman was aghast! He paid the little man and asked before the listening audience, "Tell us, what is the secret of your strength?"

"Consistent practice," said the man. "I have been the treasurer of the Baptist church downtown for the past thirty-five years."

✦✦✦✦✦✦

G

57. Gentleness

A young man decided to travel throughout Europe, so he left his most prized possession—a Tabby cat—with his brother. He gave detailed instructions about Tabby's care because he dearly loved this fur ball of purr. He had been gone several days, when he called his brother from France saying, "How's Tabby doing?"

"Oh," his brother answered, "Tabby is dead."

"What? How did.... Why would you tell me this so coldly? You know how much I loved that cat. The least you could have done was lead me up to it rather than dumping it all on me at once. I mean, you could have told me the first day I called that Tabby was on the roof. The next time you could have told me that the Fire Department was there getting her off. The next day you could have told me that even with best efforts, Tabby had died. I think this would have made it easier for me to handle. By the way, how's Mom doing?"

The brother replied, "Well, she's on the roof, but the Fire Department is on its way to get her off!"

✦✦✦✦✦✦

58. Getting on My Nerves

A rambunctious little Johnny was enjoying his very first airplane ride although no one else on the flight was enjoying it with him. He was flying alone, and the stewardess was having a very difficult time controlling the ball of energy. He was pushing every button in sight, climbing over people, and running the aisle at lightning speed. All of this kept up until the stewardess was about at her wits end.

Bringing out the coffee tray, she began serving the passengers when little Johnny came barreling down the aisle, crashed into her, sending her to the floor and the hot beverage over some of the passengers. A commotion ensued, and as Johnny hurdled over the downed stewardess, she caught him by the arm. She looked the little rascal square in the eyes, speaking so determined yet sweetly, "Little boy," she said, "why don't you go outside and play!"

✦✦✦✦✦✦

59. Getting What You Want

Little Timothy went to a friend's birthday party, but his mother had instructed him to be on his best behavior and manners. Once he returned home, his mother was inquisitive about his actions.

Mother: Now Timothy, did you do all that I asked of you?
Timothy: Yes Mother, just like you told me.
Mother: How many pieces of cake did you have?
Timothy: Three, Mother.
Mother: But Tim, I told you not to ask for another piece.
Timothy: I didn't, honest. All I told Mrs. Schlepworth is that I would love to have the recipe so my mother could make more when I got home. She gave me two more pieces all on her own!

✦✦✦✦✦✦

60. Ghostly Image

A world-renown photographer was challenged to get a photograph like none other that had been taken. He had been told that a ghostly apparition appeared every one hundred years at a local historical site. The photographer got all of his equipment together and went to the old house on the day prescribed. He waited until midnight, and sure enough the ghost appeared before him very clearly.

He struck up a conversation with the ghost and found it to be quite friendly. The ghost agreed to pose for a picture, so the photographer adjusted the flash and took the shot. Once he arrived home, the photographer downloaded his pictures from that memorable night; however, all of the shots were underexposed. Moral of the story: The spirit was willing but the flash was weak.

✦✦✦✦✦✦

61. Going Nowhere Fast

A airline flight was about midway of its destination flight time, and everything seemed to be in good shape as far as the passengers were concerned. The intercom of the jumbo jet came on, and the captain announced, "Now folks, there is no cause for alarm; however, I do feel it necessary to let you know of our situation. For the last two hours of our flight, we have been flying without the use of our radio; so, we have not been able to contact any ground stations or airports. Also, something has happened to our magnetic compass. This wasn't so bad, but about an hour ago we lost both our radar and navigational beam. What I'm trying to tell you is that I am not quite sure where we are or where we're going; however, you'll be pleased to know that we are making excellent time."

✦✦✦✦✦✦

62.   Going Out

During the middle of tornado season, a twister began to quickly move its way across the Kansas country side. Just at the crack of dawn, an old farmer spotted the tornado approaching the house. He yelled for his wife, but by this time the wind pulled the roof right off the house. It disappeared into the spiraling wind. They both jumped into the bathtub for protection, but no sooner had they done so that the wind picked up the tub sending them reeling into the sky.

Amazingly enough, the tub landed in the next county, the wind setting them down very gently. The old woman began to cry. "Don't cry, Ma," said the old farmer, "We're okay. We're not hurt."

"I know, Pa," she said still sobbing between each breath. "I just remembered that this is the first time in over twenty years that we've gone out together!"

✦✦✦✦✦✦

63.   Good Deeds

A Cub Scout troop had been trained by its den mother to do a good deed every day. Although the youngsters were willing, they were not always able to think of a new good deed for each day. Having been instructed by the den mother to attempt some deed as a troop, the little soldiers of kindness set out to complete their mission.

After some time, the den mother became quite concerned because the scouts had been gone for a long time. Finally, to the relief of their leader, the young lads returned.

"Why are you so late?" asked the den mother.

"Oh," said the troop leader, "we were helping an old man across the street, and it took us a little longer than we expected."

"That is a great thing for little Scouts to do," she said. But as the den mother began to think, she continued, "However, the troop took a great deal of time; in fact, you are over a half hour late! Why did it take so long?"

"Well, you see," said the leader, "he didn't want to go!"

64. Good Old Age

Patient: Doctor, I am concerned about doing everything necessary to live to a good old age, perhaps to 100.

Doctor: My best prescription for you is to refrain from eating chocolate, cookies, breads, and ice cream. In fact, you will need to stop eating all red meats, potatoes, and soft drinks also.

Patient: And will that help me to live to 100 years old?

Doctor: Probably not, but it will definitely make it seem like it.

✦✦✦✦✦✦

65. Good Witness

A man had been witness to an alley-way fight and had agreed to testify in the court trial. A robber had attacked a man and in the fracas had bitten the other man's ear off. Eventually after being called to the stand, the defense attorney began to cross examine the witness unmercifully.

Lawyer: Now please tell the court, how far away were you from the brawl where you allege to have seen my client?

Witness: Oh, about one hundred feet I guess.

Lawyer: And did you have your glasses on the night in question?

Witness: No, I didn't.

Lawyer: Tell me, without your glasses in the darkness, how far away can you see?

Witness: Well, I can see the moon and the stars. How far away are they?

Lawyer: (After the judge calls order back to the courtroom . . .) And to tell the truth, you could not have seen well enough the night in question to identify my client as fighting or to see my client bite off the ear of the victim, could you?

Witness: Well, I really never saw him doing either.

Lawyer: (Angrily) If it please the court, would you please tell us what you are a witness of then?

Witness: Though I didn't see him bite off the ear of that poor fellow, I was there when he spit it out.

✦✦✦✦✦✦

66. Grace Before Meals

A old farmer had come into town for some farm supplies, and while there, he decided to go to the local restaurant for lunch. When his order arrived, he quietly bowed his head and thanked the Lord for His blessings and for the provision of the food before him.

Some young men of the baser sort were sitting nearby and saw the farmer pray over his food. Desiring to make fun of the old man, they began to laugh and ridicule him. Finally, one spoke to him saying, "Hey, farmer man, does everyone back on the farm pray for his food like that?"

The farmer very kindly but pointedly replied, "Well, no son, the pigs never do!"

✦✦✦✦✦✦

67. Grandpa's Religion

During a revival meeting, a young girl gave her heart to Christ and was saved. She was excited about the transformation in her life, and she went from place to place exuberant with her newfound happiness. She ran through her house praising the Lord, singing, and leaping for joy. As she came by her cantankerous grandfather, he reproved her actions saying, "You little whippersnapper. You should be ashamed of yourself going around this house like a court jester instead of acting like a refined, young lady!"

Hearing that from her grandfather, she was devastated. She ran from the house in tears and went to the barn in back of the house. She climbed on the corral fence and saw their old mule standing close by. The bleary-eyed old mule had a sad and droopy face. The girl went over to the mule and patted her on the head, and she said with care, "Please don't cry, Bessie; I just guess you've got the same old religion that Grandpa has!"

✦✦✦✦✦✦

H

68. Happy Ending

A little boy had been begging for a puppy, and finally, Mom and Dad agreed to let him get one. The little boy could hardly contain his excitement as Dad took him to the dog kennel to look over the little dogs that needed a home. Father and child looked for a few minutes at the many dogs available.

Dad asked the boy, "Okay, son, which puppy do you want?" Without hesitation, the boy pointed to a pup that was wagging his tail so hard that his whole body moved left and right. He said, "That one there, Daddy, the one with the happy ending."

✦✦✦✦✦✦

69. Hastiness

The CEO of a major corporation was touring one of his largest production facilities with the plant's management staff. He was impressed with the hard workers and top production being accomplished through the factory. As they neared the shipping department, the CEO saw a young man lying on some boxes near the loading dock. The CEO led his entire entourage over to the young man who was obviously unconcerned about this group of managers coming towards him.

The CEO was infuriated, and he blurted out to the young man, "Hey, you there! How much money do you make a week?"

"Who me?" said the young man?

"Yes, you!" How much do you make a week?"

"Well, close to $300 a week," he said.

The CEO turned to the plant manager and said, "Have the accounting department cut a check right now for $300 to this fellow and get him out of this plant and off this property!"

The plant manager tried to butt in, "But sir . . . ."

"Don't argue with me," he said, "give him his money and get him out here now!"

Later that day the CEO received a call from the plant's accounting manager saying, "Sir, to what account would you have us to bill the $300 payment to the young man made earlier in the day?"

"Do I have to explain everything?" shouted out the executive in anger. "Bill it to payroll, of course!"

"But Sir," the accountant said, "that man didn't work for us. He was simply waiting for a signed delivery receipt."

✦✦✦✦✦✦

70. Haystack

The pastor was introducing the evangelist for the week's meeting, and he went on to explain the full meaning of the man's name. "It is so good to have Evangelist Samuel H. Thorndike with us for our revival meeting this week. I have known this man and his family for some time; as a matter of fact, we grew up not far from each other. I also know that the letter 'H' in his middle name stands for 'Haystack.' Now, while growing up, Brother Thorndike would never tell us boys what the 'H' stood for, so one day, I asked his father about it, and he is the one who told me. So, I asked his father why he would give his son a middle name like 'Haystack.' He said that when Samuel was born, he and his wife looked at him and said in unison, 'This is the last straw!'"

✦✦✦✦✦✦

71. Hearing What You Want

A man received a long distance call from a friend.

Todd:	Hello?
Operator:	You have a collect call from a Mr. Justin Jones. Will you accept the charges?
Todd:	Yes.
Justin:	Hi Todd! Thanks for taking my call.
Todd:	Sure.
Justin:	Look, I'm in the next state, and I've run out of money.
Todd:	That's tough.
Justin:	Yeah. Look, I need you to send me $200 as soon as possible.
Todd:	What was that Justin? I think we've got a bad connection.
Justin:	I said, I need for you to send me $200 as soon as possible.
Todd:	I'm sorry, Justin, I still can't hear you.
Operator:	(coming on the line) Sir, I can hear your party very clearly.
Todd:	Well then, you send him the $200.

72. Henpecked

A city-wide family conference was being conducted at the county stadium. Thousands of husbands and wives had registered to learn how to better their marriages. In order to enter the stadium, two gates had been prepared for the men to enter, to register, and to receive handout materials.

The name board over one gate stated, "Henpecked Husbands"; this gate had an almost endless line of men standing there. Looking down the line, there were pastors, politicians, and laymen who were known for their leadership abilities and powerful influence. By all appearances, the men in this line were strong and decisive, yet obviously "henpecked."

The other gate had a sign board above it stating, "Husbands Who Are Not Henpecked." At this gate, only one man stood waiting to go in. He was a frail looking man, small in stature and very soft spoken. One of the conference organizers could contain his curiosity no longer, so he went to the little man and questioned him. "Tell me sir, are you sure you're in the right line?" He replied, "Well,... ah,... yes, (he kept looking around left and right) ... all I'm doing is standing where my wife told me I should."

✦✦✦✦✦✦

73. Hereafter

An elderly woman was faithful in attending church, and in her latter years, she depended very much on the advice of her caring pastor. During a pastoral visit, he asked the lady that since she was getting on up in years, if she thought more about "the hereafter." She told him, "Oh yes, Pastor. I think about at least several times each day."

"That is wonderful," the pastor replied. "That is certainly a very wise thing to do."

"Oh pastor, it's really not a matter of wisdom. It's when I go in a room, or open a closet door, or open the refrigerator, I am always asking myself, 'What am I here after?'"

✦✦✦✦✦✦

74. Herod's Answer

During an adult Bible study, the class leader suggested that the group consider the destructive decisions made by certain Bible characters. One such character who came under scrutiny of the class was Herod and the decision he made to let Herodias' daughter ask for anything up to half his kingdom, just for dancing before him.

As an exercise, the Bible leader asked for each student to silently consider what he or she could have done to resolve the problem of Herod when the daughter requested the head of John the Baptist. Each student considered the problem, but one student spoke out with the best answer, "If I were Herod, I would have simply told her that John the Baptist was not in the half of the kingdom I offered her."

✦✦✦✦✦✦

75. He Won't Bite

A farmer had just driven downtown and parked his truck along the curbing. Getting out and going over to the parking meter, he began to put the needed money into the meter. A city man walking along the sidewalk noticed the beautiful dog sitting next to the farmer by the meter.

"What a splendid looking dog!" said the city man. The farmer looking down at the animal replied, "Yep." "Tell me, does your dog bite?" "Nope," replied the farmer, "never has to my knowledge."

With that, the city man reached down to pet the dog, when unexpectedly the dog attacked him chewing up his suit and blooding his arm. The farmer did what he could to help the stranger get the dog off of him. Once the dog had been restrained, the city man cried out, "I thought you said that your dog doesn't bite!"

"Yep," replied the farmer, "but that's not my dog!"

✦✦✦✦✦✦

76. Holes in the Head

Two local pastors were talking, and each was complaining about how bad he felt. Each was also trying to make the other feel sorrow for him by spinning a greater tale of woes.

Pastor 1:	Oh, you just don't know how bad I feel.
Pastor 2:	I should say that I do, for I know that I feel worse than you.
Pastor 1:	There's no way. I have a splitting headache.
Pastor 2:	But my head feels like I've got a hole in it.
Pastor 1:	Maybe so, but my head feels like I've got two holes in it.
Pastor 2:	That's what I hate about you so much. You've always been a "holier-than-thou" person.

77. Hopeful Proposals

Five young college ladies were talking together at a lunch table in the university dinning hall. The subject matter concerned what kind of man each would like to marry and the benefits the marriage would bring.

Sarah: I want to marry a *doctor* so that I can get medical attention for nothing.
Jill: I want to marry a *grocery store owner* so I can get food for nothing.
Kim: I want to marry a *fashion designer* so I can get new clothes for nothing.
Susie: I want to marry a *health club owner* so I can work out for nothing.
Carol: I want to marry a *preacher* so I can be good for nothing.

✦✦✦✦✦✦

78. How to Get a Crowd

There was an older businessman who was important in business circles but who was also well known for his harsh demeanor to those with whom he worked. This man came to an untimely death, and his obituary was published in the city newspaper. Two of his "friends" saw the notice and decided to attend the funeral.

When they arrived at the prescribed time, the "friends" were somewhat surprised at what they saw, for the church building was filled to capacity. One said, "This is unbelievable! Look at the number of people present for his funeral. How do you explain such a turnout?"

"Well," said the other, "give people what they want, and you can't keep them away."

✦✦✦✦✦✦

I

79. I Knew It

A traffic accident had taken place downtown, and a good citizen who had witnessed it was called to court to tell what he had seen. The court transcript read like this:

Lawyer: Did you indeed see the accident yourself?
Witness: Yes, I did.
Lawyer: Tell me, just how far away from the scene were you when you witnessed this accident?
Witness: I was standing North-North-East, thirty-six feet, seven and three quarter inches from the right corner panel of the victim's car.
Lawyer: (Believing he had the witness in a trap): Well, please tell the court just how you knew it was exactly the distance and direction you mentioned?
Witness: Because when the accident happened, I took out a compass and a tape to measure it. I knew some smart-aleck lawyer would ask me that question.

✦✦✦✦✦✦

80. Ill-Informed

A man was speaking with a friend who happened to be a rare-book collector. He told his friend about a Bible he had found in his attic, that had been in his family for generations evidently. He mentioned to his friend that it was printed by Guten-something.

His friend's face lit up, "Not Gutenberg?" he asked.

"Yes, that was the name, Gutenberg; but after seeing its condition, I just threw it away."

"Are you crazy?" the friend blurted out in disbelief. "You just threw away one of the most prized first edition books ever printed! Not long ago, a copy of a Gutenberg Bible auctioned for over $400,000!"

"Oh mine wasn't worth anything," the man said. "Nearly every page had been scribbled on by some guy named Martin Luther."

✦✦✦✦✦✦

81.   Illiterate

A man came home and found his little boy crying uncontrollably. He tried to get him calmed down enough to talk to him. "What's wrong, son?" asked Jimmy's father.

Through the tears and sniffles, the little boy explained, "Daddy, Spot is gone! Spot is gone! I've looked everywhere for him, and my little puppy is gone!" Jimmy started to cry again.

The father gets Jimmy calmed down again and then suggests, "Well, don't cry anymore, Jimmy. We'll find your puppy. We'll even put a special ad in the paper."

Jimmy began to scream more than ever at this announcement. "That won't help at all," caterwauled Jimmy, "Spot can't read!"

❖❖❖❖❖❖

82.   Imitation

Suzie:	Gramps, I didn't know you could do imitations.
Gramps:	Well, sweetheart, I don't really know that I can.
Suzie:	But can't you make out like a frog?
Gramps:	I . . . guess I could; I'm not really sure.
Suzie:	That's funny. Mommy says you can.
Gramps:	How's that, sweetheart?
Suzie:	Well, she was saying just the other day that we'll have lots of money when you croak.

❖❖❖❖❖❖

83.   Impossible Invention

An Eskimo inventor, in trying to make life more bearable for his people in the frozen tundra, invented a special Kayak. He patented a means of placing small oil heaters in the Kayak, especially around the feet. A wilderness supply company bought rights to the patent and began to manufacture the heated Kayaks.

Soon after production, the company discovered that because of the oil heaters, a majority of the crafts broke out into flames. The risk factor was too high to continue production. A spokesman for the company released the following statement to the newspapers, "We realize that you can't have a Kayak and heat it too."

❖❖❖❖❖❖

Humorous Stories

84. In a Manner of Speaking

A handy man was going house to house attempting to sell his services for money or food. One neighborhood lady, a retired English teacher, hired the man to do some odd jobs around the yard and house, and she promised to provide him with his meals as well as an hourly wage. He worked around the house for about three hours when it came time for lunch. When he knocked on the back door, the lady of the house came out and said, "And did you not notice that big pile of wood over there!"

"Yeah lady," he said, "I seen it."

"Mind your grammar!" she retorted, "You should say, 'I saw it.'"

"Well lady," he returned, "by looks of it, nobody dun saw it yet, but if you gonna saw it, no need fer me to."

"No," she said, "You should say, 'You saw it.'"

"Lady," the man replied, "I wish you'd make up your mind, but I'll tell you this. You may have saw me see it, but you've yet to see me saw it."

✦✦✦✦✦✦

85. In Control

Horace Taft was the head of the Taft School in Watertown, Connecticut. Back in the 1920's, he expelled a boy for repeatedly breaking the rules of the school as well as consistently revealing bad behavior and character. The boy's father was infuriated by Taft's action. So he wrote him, and while using numbers of expletives, he made the following statement in the letter, "You seem to think that you can run this school any way you please."

Taft returned a letter to the parent stating, "Your manners are as bad as your son, your language is coarse, but you do seem to have grasped the main idea."

✦✦✦✦✦✦

86. In the Middle

Deacon Forsythe had been married twice and now widowed twice. Both wives had been buried in the family burial plot, but Brother Forsythe decided he might better have a talk with the funeral director before his own death. They both stood at the burial site as the deacon explained,

"Sir, one of these days, you're gonna bury me in my grave here in the family plot. As you can notice, I have my two wives buried here. My first wife, Gertrude, is here on our left, and my second wife, Matilda, is here on our right. Also as you can see, there is just enough room between my wives to bury me. Now, it is very important that when you come to dig my grave and place my coffin in it, that you place me precisely equal distance between them. I want you to get out a tape and measure the distance exactly so there is no mistake; there must be complete equality. The reason for this is because I loved Gertrude as much as I did Matilda and Matilda as much as I did Gertrude. (After a moment's contemplation): But, now that I reflect on it, if you happen to make a little mistake in the measuring, then, if you would, lean me a little toward Matilda!"

✦✦✦✦✦✦

87. Indian Appraisal

An Indian chief was invited to attend a revival meeting. He had never gone to one, so he decided to do so just to see what the service was like. When the evangelistic services came to the town nearby his settlement, he came to hear the preacher. Very quietly and with intense interest, the chief listened to every word the man said.

When the service was completed, a friend asked him what he thought of the evangelist. The chief replied, "Much wind—plenty thunder—no rain!"

✦✦✦✦✦✦

88. Innovation

During the Black Hawk war (a conflict between the United States and the Sac and Fox Indians in 1832), Abraham Lincoln (1809-1865) was a very young captain of a group known as the Bucktail Rangers. Because Lincoln was unaware of many finer points of military tactics, drill, and platoon formations, he consistently faced a difficulty as they marched across the country.

When his company would come to a fence and locked gate, he did not know how to command them to get over it in a refined, military way. All he knew to do was to give the command, "Company, Halt! Dismissed for two minutes. At the end of that time, fall in on the other side of the fence."

✦✦✦✦✦✦

89. Insomnia

A woman had been having a little problem and since she did not know how to handle it herself, she decided to go to a psychiatrist.

Psychiatrist: Tell me now, what seems to be the problem?
Woman: Mainly, I have been unable to sleep at night.
Psychiatrist: Well, that's not an uncommon problem. Many people have insomnia. Perhaps you might try some sleeping aid.
Woman: Doctor, the problem is more complicated than that.
Psychiatrist: How so?
Woman: Well, it's like this. The main problem is that my husband thinks he is a refrigerator.
Psychiatrist: Is that so? This is very unusual. Don't you think your husband should be the one here for a visit?
Woman: Oh no, I'm okay with that. The problem is that he sleeps at night with his mouth open, and the light keeps me awake.

✦✦✦✦✦✦

90. Intense Desire

Janie, a little girl of four years, was in bed upstairs. She called out to her dad who was relaxing in the den downstairs. With the house somewhat quiet, her father could hear Janie from her bedroom.

Janie: Will you bring me a drink of water?
Dad: No, Janie, you have already had your drink of water. Go to sleep.

About five minutes passed when the conversation repeated.

Janie: Daddy, will you bring me a drink of water?
Dad: No, Janie. As I told you, you have already had enough water. Go to sleep. Now, don't call down again.

Another five minutes passed.

Janie: Daddy, please bring me a drink of water.
Dad: Janie, if you don't quit calling down for water, I will have to come up and spank you.

Another five minutes passed.

Janie: Daddy, when you come to spank me, will you bring me a drink of water.

✦✦✦✦✦✦

91.   I've Had Enough

A man was walking downtown when he decided to take a short-cut through an alley. No sooner had he turned the corner than a robber stuck a gun in his back, demanding all his money. The man immediately grabbed the gun, tossed it in a nearby dumpster, and commenced to beat up the would-be robber. He blackened his eyes, broke his arm, cracked his ribs, dislocated his jaw, and knocked out several teeth. While lying on the ground in a heap of broken flesh and seeing the man come after him again, the robber cried out, "Hey mister. Aren't you ever gonna call the police?"

✦✦✦✦✦✦

J

92. Job Qualifications

A downtown business was in need of a unique worker in the office. The owner placed ads in the paper and on a sign-board in the window of his office. Several days passed, but no one had answered the ads or even asked about the sign in the window until a German Shepherd came in the front office with the sign board in his mouth. The dog readily found the owner, giving him the sign. A typed note on the dog's collar was the indication that he wanted the advertised job. The owner thought this was quite strange, but since no one else had inquired about the job, he thought to at least conduct the interview.

He told the dog that there were three basic requirements that needed to be met in order to get the job. "First, the employee must be able to type at least sixty words a minute with no mistakes," he said. The Shepherd immediately jumped up on the chair behind the latest computer word-processor and began typing away at ninety words per minute. In no time, a perfect letter came from the printer. The dog took it and handed it to the owner.

The owner went on to give the second requirement. He told the dog that the employee needed must be a skilled office filer. Seeing a stack of folders that needed filing, the German Shepherd grabbed the stack of folders and like a whirlwind went to the filing cabinet putting files in place with lightning speed. The owner looked in the file drawers and saw that the work had been done flawlessly.

"Now," the owner said, "I'm quite surprised but impressed with your skills, Mr. Shepherd. There is only one more requirement that you must meet, but it might be quite hard." The dog barked as an indication that he was ready for the challenge. The owner went on, "The last requirement is that this employee must be bi-lingual." The dog looked straight at the owner and said confidently, "Meow."

✦✦✦✦✦✦

93. Just a Matter of Time

A young mother and her five-year old son came by the house to visit a friend and her husband, who happened to be doctor. The young mother made no obvious attempts to restrain the rambunctious activities of her son; consequently, he went from room to room playing with everything he saw. As the adults were talking, the clatter of bottles could be heard in the doctor's personal office just off from the living room.

The mother said, "I hope you don't mind little Johnny making all that noise in your office, doctor." The doctor replied, "Oh, that's no problem. He'll quiet down when he gets to the poisons."

❖❖❖❖❖❖

K

94. Keep Feeding Her

Little three-year-old Janie was into her usual antics of testing and trying out new experiences. As Janie's mother was cleaning the house, she saw the three-year-old pick up a nickel, inspect it closely, and straightway swallow it. Quite terrified at what she saw, the mother hurried to Janie, turned her upside down, and started to shake her while pounding her back. During all this commotion, Janie coughed up two dimes.

Mother was frantic at this point, and she called to her husband, "Hurry! Quick! Janie swallowed a nickel and just coughed up two dimes! What are we going to do?"

The father yelled back quickly, "We can use the extra money! Keep feeding her nickels!"

✦✦✦✦✦✦

95. Keeping Silence

An old-time preacher was moderating a business meeting when a woman got up and began to speak. This offended the preacher because he didn't believe that women should speak in the church but rather keep silence. Interrupting her, he said, "Sister, Paul did say in the Scripture that it is unlawful for a woman to speak in the church, so I must demand that you take a seat and keep silent."

The woman responded saying, "Well now Preacher, if you believe that way, you just tell me where would you men be if it weren't for women?"

The preacher quickly replied, "In the Garden of Eden, Sister, in the Garden of Eden!"

✦✦✦✦✦✦

96. Keeping Your Word

A conversation took place between a customer and the owner of a bait and tackle shop.

Customer: I would like to buy some cockroaches. Tell me, do you carry them here?

Owner:	Why, yes, we do. We sell them to fishermen for bait.
Customer:	Great, I'd like to have 10,000 of them please.
Owner:	I believe we can fill the order, but let me ask, why do you want so many?
Customer:	I'm moving from my apartment, and my lease requires me to leave it in the same condition I found it.

✦✦✦✦✦✦

97. Knowing What to Say

A young preacher had been having an especially difficult time in knowing exactly what to say in the first seconds of his messages. Specifically, he did not know how to introduce himself and his theme to the audience. The problem for him was so urgent that he had become quite nervous about any speaking engagement, even to the point of complete terror. He asked many of his friends and had gotten some advice. In different settings, he began to try a variety of the recommendations. For the most part, these had become successful. At least he had somewhat overcome most of the initial nervousness.

The young preacher was soon asked to speak in a Federal prison for the criminally insane. Although this was certainly an unusual place for him to hold a speaking engagement, he believed his message important enough to speak there.

The moment arrived when he stood before the unusual congregation, and he began with his learned introductory statements. He began, "Fellow citizens"—but being Federal prisoners, he immediately knew that was not right. He began to get nervous but continued with another introduction, "Fellow convicts"—but this received a snicker of laughs from the inmates.

Finally trying the most conventional means he could think of as an introduction, he said, "I'm so glad to see so many of you here tonight." After that, the whole group broke out in uncontrollable laughter.

In disgust, the young preacher used the only generic introduction he had been taught just to get right into his message. He said, "Why are we all here tonight?" From the back of the auditorium came a reply from one of the inmates, "Because we aren't all there!"

✦✦✦✦✦✦

98. Knowing Your Place

All the children of the elementary grades were assigned to write a brief history of their families; among the children was the young daughter of William Howard Taft, III. This is what she wrote: "My great-grandfather held the position of the twenty-seventh President of the United States. My grandfather, Robert Alphonso Taft, was a Senator from Ohio. My father is the Ambassador to Ireland. I am a Brownie."

✦✦✦✦✦✦

L

99. Late and In a Hurry

A young girl was on her way to Sunday school but running a little late. Wanting to make sure she kept her perfect attendance record in tact, she talked to the Lord very earnestly as she ran, praying, "Dear Lord, I don't want to be late! Please help me, Lord, not to be late! Help me to hurry." Just as she got that prayer from her lips, she tripped and fell. She got up, brushed herself off, but noticed that her knee was scraped and her dress was torn. Again she began running and praying. "Dear Lord, I don't want to be late! Please help me not to be late, but Lord, please don't shove me either."

❖❖❖❖❖❖

100. Learning Politeness

Back in the days of the sometimes wild west, a young mother was attempting to bring up her little boy with a little more grace and politeness than that which was going on around them. However, the little boy was having a difficult time learning some of the lessons of gentlemanly behavior. The boy was especially enthralled by the bow-legged cowboys who would walk down the street, so much so that he could hardly contain his wonder.

One day when he and his mother were store shopping, the tyke saw the cowboys coming and as they got in his presence, he yelled out, "Mother, Mother! Look at those bow-legged cowboys!" This embarrassed his mother terribly, so they immediately went home where she could have a good talk with him. He seemed to understand the problem and agreed not to do it again.

The next week, the mother and child were in town again when the cowboys began to approach down the plank sidewalk. The boy looked up and yelled, "Mother, Mother! Look coming yonder. Those are bow-legged cowboys!" Again his mother was embarrassed but now determined to teach him better than the rudeness he had been showing. So, she took him home and demanded that he spend his days reading Shakespeare. He was to do this all day for three weeks before he would be allowed to return to town. She explained to him that perhaps this would help his speech be a little more becoming of a young gentleman.

The time passed, the child did as directed by his mother, and the day came for the mother and child to return to town. Sure enough, as they traversed the street, here came the bow-legged cowboys. The mother watched and listened intently to see what her son would do. He looked at the men and then at his mother. He said with dignity, "Hark, Mother! What manner of men are these, who wear their knees in parentheses?"

✦✦✦✦✦✦

101. Listening to What You're Told

A loner of a man had become accustomed to being by himself, but it was extremely lonely. In order to make life a little more bearable, he purchased a tabby cat for company. To make the cat even more company, he tried teaching Tabby to speak. He used tuna and salmon treats as rewards for her efforts in the speaking lessons, but even after several years, she had never breathed a word.

After a long speech-therapy class, Tabby was enjoying one of her "fishy" treats when she looked up at her owner and screamed, "Look out! Look out!" The owner never responded other than to look at Tabby in amazement. Suddenly the ceiling fell on the head of the owner. Looking at her knocked-out owner, Tabby said, "Three years of teaching me to speak and then you won't even listen to what I have to say."

✦✦✦✦✦✦

102. Logic Problem

It has been reported that the town council in County Cork, Ireland, had a great deal of trouble with criminals. Not only that, their town jail was filled to capacity, and they needed a new jail. Because the town was low on funds for new construction, the council proposed a three-step resolution to the problem. It was presented as follows:
(1)   The town will build a new jail.
(2)   The new jail will be constructed by using the materials from the old jail.
(3)   The old jail shall be used until the new jail has been completed.

✦✦✦✦✦✦

103. Looking Back

During Sunday school class, the teacher was describing the story of Lot escaping from Sodom and Gomorrah with his family. She went on to describe how

God had told the family not even to look back at the city when the fire and brimstone fell from heaven on those wicked cities. When the teacher got to the place in the story where Lot's wife looked back, she said, "Lot's wife looked back, and she turned into a pillar of salt!"

Little Zach immediately raised his hand and blurted out, "That's nothing! My mother looked back one time while driving, and she turned into a telephone pole!"

✦✦✦✦✦✦

104. Lord Knows

William Lyons Phelps (1865-1943) was a professor of English at Yale University. Once, on a pre-Christmas examination on English literature, a student turned in a very short response to the examination question by stating, "The Lord only knows the answer to this question. Merry Christmas!"

After the Christmas break, the student received his test from Professor Phelps with this note attached, "The Lord gets an A; you get an F. Happy New Year!"

✦✦✦✦✦✦

105. Lot to be Thankful For

A tenth chief justice, Melville W. Fuller (1833-1910), was leading a church meeting when someone in the congregation began to rail against higher education, colleges, and universities. The man braggingly announced, "I thank God that I have never been corrupted through any association with a college!"

Fuller responded, "Do we hear you correctly sir, that you are thanking the Lord for your ignorance?"

The man replied, "I guess, if you want to put it that way, yes, I am."

"Therefore," said Fuller, "we would be agreed that you have a great deal to be thankful for!"

✦✦✦✦✦✦

106. Love for Children

A famous child psychologist, known for his great love for children, had spent a great deal of time laying a new cement sidewalk around his house and gardens. After finishing the job, he was admiring his work from inside while the cement was setting. Suddenly, his wife saw him fly off in an almost uncontrollable rage, for some children had begun to draw on his walkways.

Just about the time he was opening the door to yell at the kids, the psychologist's wife called to him, "But remember, darling, you love children."

"Yes, I know," he said as he opened the door to leave, "I love them in the abstract, but not in the concrete!"

❖❖❖❖❖❖

107. Lying

A little girl was facing a moral dilemma in her young life. Her teacher, her pastor, and her parents were teaching her that telling a lie is sinful. On the other hand, she was troubled, for she was discovering just how difficult it was not to tell a lie from time to time. In order to resolve the conflict going on in her mind, she determined to begin her own investigation. First, she started with her Father.

Girl:	Father, have you ever told a lie?
Father:	Well, if I were to say that I have never lied, then I would have told a lie.
Girl:	What about Mother? Has she lied?
Father:	I guess, when she felt that perhaps the truth would have hurt, I suppose she has lied.
Girl:	Well, what about Grandpa?
Father:	I reckon, he has.
Girl:	And Grandma too?
Father:	I assume she's just like the rest of us. If the circumstances seemed to—
Girl:	(Interrupting): Father, you know, Heaven must be a really lonely place—with no one up there but God and George Washington!

❖❖❖❖❖❖

M

108. Man in Charge

Someone called the church office, and while speaking to the secretary said, "Let me speak to the head hog at the trough."

Shocked and appalled, the serious-minded church secretary reprimanded the caller saying, "How dare you speak of our pastor in such a manner? He is a man of God and deserves respect for the great man that he is."

"Sorry lady," the caller replied, "I was simply calling in to donate $100,000 to your ministry."

She responded quickly, "If you can wait just a couple of seconds, I think I hear the big fat pig coming right now."

✦✦✦✦✦✦

109. Man or a Mouse?

Sam and David were good friends at college but had lost touch over the years. One day, the two happened upon each other, and they began to reminisce the "good ole days" as well as catch up on the events current in their lives. They spoke of their families but especially about their wives. David spoke boldly to Sam, "What are you, Sam, a man or a mouse?"

"Why, there's no doubt. I'm a man," Sam replied.

"What makes you think that so confidently?" David asked.

"'Cause," Sam answered, "my wife is afraid of a mouse!"

✦✦✦✦✦✦

110. Many Marriages

Sarah:	Oh, Michelle, I am so looking forward to getting married.
Michelle:	Really? What's made you so excited about it?
Sarah:	I've just come to realize that I'm going to have sixteen husbands.
Michelle:	Sixteen? You can only have one husband!
Sarah:	No. I'm going to have sixteen. I heard the preacher say it was okay.
Michelle:	Are you sure that's what the preacher said?
Sarah:	Of course. I was at a wedding the other day, and he said, "Four better, four worse, four richer, and four poorer."

111. Marital Paradise

The marriage relationship of Adam and Eve was truly a model of paradise, mainly for two reasons: (1) Adam never had to hear from Eve about all the men she could have married instead, and (2) Eve never had to listen to Adam go on about the marvelous ways his mother cooked meals.

✦✦✦✦✦✦

112. Matter of Perspective

A young girl had gone to Sunday school for the very first time, and she was fascinated by the stories she heard from the teacher. Once the family got in the car, returning home, the little lady said, "Dad, I have a question about what was taught in our lesson today."

"Sure, Honey," he said, "what do you want to know?"

"Well, the teacher read from the Bible today about all the Children of Israel did. The Children of Israel crossed the Red Sea, the Children of Israel built the Tabernacle, and the Children of Israel made sacrifices to God. What I want to know is, did the grown-ups ever do anything?"

✦✦✦✦✦✦

113. Mellow Voice

One of the soloists of the church was quite pleased with himself following one of his specials in the morning service. A church member commented, "Your voice quality is hard to describe. I would say that it is very mellow." The solist took this to be an accolade of his ability until he went home and looked up the word "mellow." The definition indicated, "over-ripe; almost rotten."

✦✦✦✦✦✦

114. Memorization

One day in the jungle, an elephant came to a nearby lake to get a drink of water. Glancing up after a big gulp, he spotted a turtle sunning himself on a log near the shore. The elephant moved slowly toward the turtle, sneaking up on him from behind. Suddenly, the elephant took one of his mighty feet and squashed the turtle into total oblivion.

A nearby monkey, seeing all that had transpired, came to the elephant and enquired, "Why did you do that? What did that turtle ever do to you?"

He replied, "Twenty years ago, I came to this lake to get a drink of water. Slipping my trunk into the water, that turtle came by and bit me."

"But how did you know that this was the same one? That's remarkable memory!"

"Absolutely," the elephant said proudly, "I have turtle recall."

✦✦✦✦✦✦

115. Memory Verse Overload

Little Bobby had been working hard on completing his Sunday school assignment of learning a list of Bible verses. For the most part, he had done a good job with his memory work, but occasionally, he would get a couple of words mixed up. As customary, Mother and Father would help Bobby by asking him to repeat his verses for them. On Thursday night, the parents sat on the edge of Bobby's bed and asked, "Did you memorize your verse for today, Bobby?" "Yes, I did," he replied, "I don't remember the reference, but it is the verse that says, 'A lie is an abomination unto the Lord but an ever present help in time of trouble.'"

✦✦✦✦✦✦

116. Merely for Others to See

A man returned from shopping to the parking lot where his brand new, red sports car was parked. As he approached it, his heart sunk as he noticed the rear quarter panel had been significantly damaged. After a few moments of near tearful emotions, he was encouraged that someone had left a piece of paper under his wiper blade. The note read as follows.

"All the people who saw me side-swipe your car are now watching me as I write this note. No doubt, they believe I am giving you my name, number, and insurance information so that I can pay for the damages. You should be so lucky."

✦✦✦✦✦✦

117. Mistaken Purpose

A gentleman came to the doctor for help regarding a sore throat. As he entered the examination area, the following conversation took place.

Patient: Doc, I've been having trouble with a sore throat. Could you help

	me?
Doctor:	Yes, I believe so. If you would, go in that room and disrobe. I'll be there in a moment to examine you.
Patient:	But Doctor, is that necessary? All that's wrong is my throat.
Doctor:	Please sir, just go in the other room, disrobe, and I'll be there momentarily to examine you.

Even though a little frustrated, the man went in the room, and disrobed to his "skivvies." Also sitting in the room was another man in the same attire who had a large package under his arm.

Patient:	Can you believe this doctor? I've come in here with a sore throat, and he's made me dress like this for an examination.
Man:	What have you got to complain about? All I came to do was deliver this package.

✦✦✦✦✦✦

118. Money for College

A college student had been overspending his cash allotment from home on many frivolous purchases. Finding himself in dire straights one month, he wrote home in hopes of cleverly getting his parents to send more money.

Dear Mom and Dad,
    A$ you know, I $incerely cheri$h all the thing$ you $acrificially a$$i$t me with at $chool. $ince I heard from you la$t, I have $ensed $ome $pecial need$ at college. I a$$ume that you will write $oon; I await your next corre$pondence with great enthuiam. I hope you ene what I am $aying.
    $incerely, Your $on, $am.

Dear Sam,
    Y◯ur m◯m and I enj◯yed getting y◯ur recent letter fr◯m c◯llege. Y◯u are ◯n ◯ur minds c◯nstantly, and y◯u will be glad t◯ kn◯w that we underst◯◯d y◯ur letter c◯mpletely. We t◯◯, l◯◯k f◯rward t◯ getting y◯ur letters at h◯me. Please write us again s◯◯n.
    L◯ve, Dad and M◯m.

✦✦✦✦✦✦

119. Musical Taste

A man had a dog who had learned to play classical piano pieces, and his specialty was Bach. To potentially acquire fame and fortune, the owner took the dog to a music producer for an audition and hopefully a recording contract. The owner did emphasize to the producer that the dog was temperamental and that at all costs, he must listen to him play very carefully else the dog would pounce on him and severely bite him.

The producer agreed, and the dog was brought in for his audition performance. He began to play, but it was obviously terrible. However, the producer sat there calmly until the canine had completed the performance. Once the dog was led from the room, the producer blurted out at the owner, "I should have stopped him early on and let him attack me, for I am most sure that his Bach is worse than his bite!"

❖❖❖❖❖❖

N

120. Name Calling

Little Laura went to her first day at school. She came to the teacher's desk to provide some simple introductory information about herself and her family.

Teacher: Laura, what is your father's name?
Laura: Daddy.
Teacher: I know, Honey, but by what name does he go by?
Laura: Daddy.
Teacher: Okay, tell me, what name does your mother call him?
Laura: Oh, she doesn't call him anything. She likes him.

✦✦✦✦✦✦

121. Near Impossible

An elderly farmer sat rocking on the front porch of his old homestead, talking with a stranger to those parts. "Been near thirty years since I lost my wife in them woods yonder."

"Oh my, I'm sorry to hear that!" said the stranger. "It must be hard to lose your wife like that."

"Hard?" the farmer bellowed. "Was near impossible. She knew those woods like the back of her hand!"

✦✦✦✦✦✦

122. Needing Help

Some sightseers were going on their very first plane ride, and they were more than a little nervous about the experience; however, the soothing and calming voice of the captain put them at ease. They really began to have confidence that the pilot had everything under control and that he would be able to handle any situation that would arise. The flight began, and the plane reached its cruising altitude of 33,000 feet.

All was going smoothly until suddenly engine number one caught fire. The plane shifted left and right while engine two raced to keep the plane in flight. Flames shot from the first engine, and everyone in the passenger's cabin began screaming for their lives, "We're on fire! We're on fire, and we're going to crash!"

Just then, the consoling voice of the captain came on the intercom. "Folks, there is no need for alarm. I will be shutting down engine number one, and this will extinguish the flames. This airliner is well able to fly with one engine. Just as a precaution, we are diverting to the nearest airport. Again, I remind you, everything is under control. There is no cause for alarm." With that news, everyone calmed down and returned to conversing with one another. Everyone agreed that they appreciated the wisdom and ability of the pilot to handle the situation.

The plane had begun to descend and was at about 28,000 feet when engine number two burst into flames. At this, the passengers once again began to scream. Some were running down the aisle shouting, "Both engines are gone! We're going to crash! We're going to crash!"

During this mayhem, the pilot came from the cockpit wearing a parachute. "Attention! Please be calm! Don't worry," he reassured them, "Everything will be fine; I'm going for help."

✦✦✦✦✦✦

123. Needing Rescue

Two men were hunting but got lost in a forest of which they were not familiar. After wandering for a couple of hours, they were no sooner to being found than at the first. Sitting on a log together, they began to discuss the problem and what was needed for them to be rescued.

Hunter 1:	First of all, we need to remain calm.
Hunter 2:	You're right. We cannot panic. Sooner or later, we will be found.
Hunter 1:	You know, I read in one of my hunting magazines that if a hunter gets lost in the woods, that he should shoot three times into the air and that someone will come and rescue him.
Hunter 2:	Really, that sounds great! Let's try it.

They did just as the first hunter suggested, but nothing happened. Not giving up, they tried it several times; however, there was still no response from anyone. Losing a little bit of hope, they once again began to talk.

Hunter 2:	What are we going to do now? No one is responding.
Hunter 1:	At this point, I don't know, because we're almost out of arrows, too.

✦✦✦✦✦✦

124. Newlywed Blues

A newlywed husband found his wife in tears, and it specifically concerned her cooking. He came to her and made every attempt to console her, but at this point nothing he said made the situation better. At the last, he finally apologized, "Honey, I'm sorry. I really did not mean that you were a bad cook. All I said was that by all indications, it appears that our garbage disposal has developed ulcers."

✦✦✦✦✦✦

125. Nightmare

By all appearances, James and Janie were sleeping comfortably until, in the wee hours of the morning, Janie suddenly began screaming at the top of her lungs. James almost had a heart attack from being awakened by this blood-curdling scream. Once he caught his breath and awakened Janie from her nightmare, he asked, "What in the world are you screaming for? You scarred me half to death!"

"Oh, James," she cried, "it was a terrible dream! I dreamt that all husbands were being auctioned away, and there was nothing we could do to stop it. Some were selling for $500, some for $1,000, some for $10,000, and still others for $100,000."

James had a little smile of pride come across his face as he thought of his own value. "And tell me, dear, how much did husbands like me go for?"

"James, that's why I screamed out so loudly!" she said, "They had cart loads of husbands like you, selling three for a dollar!"

✦✦✦✦✦✦

126. No Enemies

A pastor was preaching a series of messages on brotherly love. Seeking an innovative approach to one of the messages, he decided to ask a question of the congregation. He asked, "Is there anyone here who can say truthfully that you don't have any enemies? If you can say this, I would like for you to stand, please."

Everyone in the congregation looked at each other, and a little nervous shuffling took place; the embarrassing tension could be felt by all. After a few moments, a ninety-three year old gentleman stood and said, "Here, pastor, me. I have no enemies."

The congregation and pastor gave the elder respect through a moment of applause. As the ovation silenced, the pastor asked the man, "Could you tell us please, what is your secret?"

"Sure, preacher," the elder replied with a grin, "I outlived all of 'em."

127. Not at Fault

Bill and Jerry were neighbors who borrowed tools and lawn equipment from each other consistently. Over the years, they had few problems with their practice, that is, until it came to Bill's discovery that his new ratchet was broken. All he could figure was that Jerry had borrowed it, returned it broken, and never told him. Bill and Jerry met over the picket fence to heatedly discuss the matter.

Bill: Alright, Jerry, when you returned my ratchet, I discovered that you had broken it. I want to know what you're going to do about it?

Jerry: Now Bill, that's not right. What you're suggesting didn't happen!

Bill: Jerry, I know you broke it.

Jerry: Let me explain it to you, Bill, because it's not my fault. (1) I never borrowed your ratchet; (2) It was in good condition when I brought it back; and (3) It was already broken when you lent it to me.

✦✦✦✦✦✦

128. Not Good Enough

A man had spent a great deal of time training bird dogs for the purpose of selling them. One dog was especially good, and the trainer took the dog on his very first trial hunt. The trainer shot a duck which fell into the water, and he commanded the dog to fetch the bird. He did so, but surprising even the trainer, the dog walked on the water, picked up the bird, and brought it back. The man was astounded but greatly pleased. He shot another bird; it too fell in the lake. Before the bird could sink, the dog calmly walked across the water and retrieved the bird.

The man now thinking he had a high-dollar dog to sale called a hard-to-please but wealthy hunter who wanted a new dog. The buyer and trainer took the dog out by the lake. After the buyer shot a duck and it falling into the water, the dog, as usual, walked on the water and brought the bird back.

The trainer said proudly, "Tell me, what do you think of this dog? Don't you want to buy him?" "No, not really," the buyer replied. "I mean, he's a nice dog, but he can't even swim."

✦✦✦✦✦✦

129. Not So Bad After All

A very popular activity in Florida is for people to take jungle-boat rides. This is an enjoyable cruise where people have to avoid the low overhanging vegetation, the snakes in the water, and the alligators along the shoreline. On one particular cruise, a patron asked the guide, "Is there ever any problems with snakes dropping in the boat from these overhanging branches."

The guide answered, "No problem at all."

"But," questioned the patron, "say that you do get a snake in the boat. Won't people be jumping overboard?"

The guide replied confidently, "Let me explain. If you get a snake in the boat, then you get people in the water. If you get people in the water, you get alligators in the water. If you get alligators in the water, then you get people who realize it's not so bad to be in the boat!"

✦✦✦✦✦✦

130. Not What it Seems

Jerry was leaving a restaurant and picked up the wrong umbrella at the door. As he was just about to leave, he was caught by a patron of the restaurant, the real owner of the umbrella he had in his hand. Jerry was so embarrassed that he had done this misdeed, even innocently, and he made his heart-felt apologies to the man.

As Jerry walked down the sidewalk, he was reminded about his family's need for umbrellas. He darted in a nearby department store and bought an umbrella for himself, his wife, and his daughter. As he was headed back down the sidewalk toward his car, Jerry met the man from the restaurant. The man looked quite cynically at Jerry and the umbrellas in his hands; he said, "Well, I see that you've had a good day after all."

✦✦✦✦✦✦

O

131. Obituaries

In these days of execution, describing how a family member who is a capital offender dies might prove embarrassing and disgraceful for the family. In order to make it sound more palatable, some of the family members might describe their loved one's untimely passing as follows:

Electrocution: He occupied the chair of applied electricity at one of our larger state-run institutions. He died in that position.

Hanging: He died in a public ceremony. Unfortunately, the platform on which he was standing gave way.

Firing Squad: He was an unfortunate recipient of a bullet to the heart. No charges were filed against the man handling the firearm, seeing that various officers were standing nearby and witnessed the incident.

Guillotine: After a long time of institutional isolation, he finally succumbed to head and neck injuries.

Gassing: He passed away due to respiratory complications.

❖❖❖❖❖❖

132. Offerings and Sacrifice

Two barnyard animals, a pig and a chicken, began to converse about their own dedication to the cause of the gospel ministry. Each one thought itself to be more spiritual than the other. Along the edge of the fence, they saw an announcement board at the nearby church that read, "Breakfast next Saturday morning. Ham and eggs." The chicken said to the pig, "Just to show you how spiritual I am, for this breakfast I will give an offering of the eggs they need." The pig snorted, "Spiritual indeed. For you, the breakfast is only an offering; for me it's complete sacrifice!"

❖❖❖❖❖❖

133. Oh Susie!

A preacher went to visit in an insane asylum. As he was walking down the corridor, he went by a man who had his head in his hands crying, "Oh Susie! Oh

Susie! Oh Susie!" The preacher asked the manager, "What's wrong for him to cry so?" "Well," he said, "this poor man lost his greatest love, Susie. She left him, and he's never gotten over the loss of that love. It has left him in this condition."

They traveled a little farther and as they passed several rooms, they came by one that was locked in several places. The room was also padded with rubber for the man's protection. As they came by the room, the preacher heard the man inside screaming and crying out uncontrollably. The inmate was yelling, "Oh Susie! Oh Susie! Oooohhhh Susie!"

The preacher peeked in the little window at the door and saw the distraught man humped over in the corner. "Why is he crying for Susie?" the preacher asked. The manager replied, "Oh, this is the man who married Susie!"

✦✦✦✦✦✦

134. Old Bore

Pastor Simmons saw a lady from the church, Sister Carol, coming up the walk to the parsonage. Intending to escape, the pastor told his wife, "You talk to her. I refuse to be bothered by her endless chatter and gossip. I'm going upstairs to study. Just tell her that I'm busy and can't come down."

About three hours had passed, and thinking he had heard Sister Carol leave, Pastor Simmons called to his wife from upstairs, "Hey, Sweetheart, is that 'old bore' left and gone home yet?"

Sister Carol still sat there with the pastor's wife in earshot of all that was said, but fortunately for the pastor, his wife was a quick-thinking lady. She replied to her husband, "Yes, dear. She's been gone for some time, and Sister Carol is here now!"

✦✦✦✦✦✦

135. Old-Fashioned Discipline

A mother and her little boy went shopping one day, and as they walked through the toy section of the department store, the boy eyed a large rocking horse. With jubilation, he climbed on the horse and rode it for over an hour. Mother, at last ready to the leave the store, asked Junior to get down from the horse so they could leave—he refused! She tried everything she knew to get him off the horse but also not to make a public scene; however, all her efforts were to no avail.

She called the store manager for help, but all his efforts to coax the lad from his stead were futile. As a last-ditch effort, a psychiatrist was called in to help the child. Once the doctor arrived he quickly assessed the situation. He stepped up beside the rocking horse and leaning up to the boy, he whispered something in his ear. Immediately, the boy leapt from the horse, ran to his mother's side, and clutched her hand.

Everyone was astounded at the amazingly quick results wielded by the psychiatrist. The store manager and mother enquired of him exactly what he had said. He reported, "All I said was, 'If you don't immediately get off this high horse your on, I'll whip the stuffing out of you!'"

✦✦✦✦✦✦

136.   Old Man, New Man

A man was arrested for the crime of breaking and entering. He was brought before the judge, and the accused excused his behavior as follows. "Your honor, I am guilty of the crime of which I am charged, but I would like to give you an understanding of the plight my life is in. You see, not long ago, I became a Christian, but I have discovered that even though I am a new man, the old man is still with me, driving me to do some things I don't want to do."

The judge replied, "I do understand what you are going through; however, this case is especially complicated by what you've just told me. Therefore, my judgment and sentencing must be fair to all the parties involved. Because this crime was planned and committed by the old man, I sentence him to sixty days in jail. Although I am inclined to give consideration to the new man, because he was an accomplice to the robbery, failing to prevent the crime, I sentence him to thirty days. Both of you must serve a combined sentence of ninety days in jail."

✦✦✦✦✦✦

137.   One for Me, One for God

A little girl was on her way to Sunday school playing with the quarters her Mom and Dad had given her. One of the shiny coins was for the offering plate at church, and one they gave for her to keep as her own.

While walking along the sidewalk at the church, she was tossing the coins in the air and catching them. She did this several times until she missed one of the quarters. It rolled along the curbing and fell into a nearby sewer grate. She knelt by the grate and saw the coin disappear into the watery depths below. She said sadly, "What a shame. There goes God's quarter."

138. Only Thirty-Two Days

A young man had stopped by a downtown café to get a bite to eat. It just so happened that this café was just a block from the local university. Many of the other patrons were college students, which made the restaurant lively with youthful energy. The young man especially noticed two college students who were elated and cheering at their table, and they were holding a box in their hands. They kept rejoicing about some accomplishment of theirs saying, "Just thirty-two days. Only thirty-two days!"

Every once in a while, another student would come in jumping up and down, giving high-fives to the others at the table, saying "Just thirty-two days. Only thirty-two days!" This happened several times until there were five college students at the table who were beside themselves with the spirit of success.

The young man could not contain his curiosity any longer, so he went over by the table. As he drew near, he noticed that the box in the middle of the table was a jig-saw puzzle, and he heard them rejoicing about how brief a time it took them to put it together. "Just thirty-two days," they said, "only thirty-two days! And this puzzle said two-to-three years!"

✦✦✦✦✦✦

139. Opportunity for a Witness

A young man had been recently converted at a very large and well-known church in the area, one whose pastor was nationally televised each week. The young man was quite zealous for opportunities of sharing his faith with others although he did not yet possess all the skills of introducing the gospel to new acquaintances. Still, he did try to find some way to take a stand for the Lord.

For his company's business, the young man had to take a plane trip from the east coast to California, and he resolved in his heart that he would witness to whomever he sat beside. When he got on the plane, he sat down next to a drunk. The young man was very unsure about how to talk to this inebriated person or how to be an effective testimony in this situation. He tried to introduce himself, something about the Lord, something about his church, and even later something about his famous pastor; however, the man practically ignored him. There were a few minutes of silence between them.

The drunk was reading the local newspaper from the area, and soon asked the young man, "Tell me, sir, why does a person get arthritis?"

Already being consumed about presenting his faith, he thought maybe he could use this as an opportunity. He responded, "Arthritis is the definite result of drinking, revelry, and wicked friends!" He was quite proud of himself but wondered saying, "Why do you ask?"

"Oh," the drunk replied, "I was just reading here in the religion section that your pastor suffers a great deal from arthritis."

❖❖❖❖❖❖

140. Optimism or Pessimism?

A young man had joined the army thinking he wanted to be a paratrooper; however, once his training began, he became deathly nervous even thinking about jumping from a perfectly good airplane. Nervous or not, it was too late. He would still have to complete his training and jump as a paratrooper.

He was sent to Fort Benning, Georgia, to train as a parachutist. He learned from the training models how to jump, pull the rip cord, fall, and roll. All of this was fine until the time came for the men to make their first jump from the plane. Everyone was lined up along the walls of the plane with their gear on, and the plane was nearing the drop sight.

The jump captain stood at the open door of the plane and reminded the men once again of the procedure they were to follow. He shouted, "Remember, when you jump from the plane, you must do so quickly from a single-file line. There must not be any hesitation at the door. As you leave the plane, you must do the following. First, count to ten by repeating the words 'One thousand one, One thousand two, etc.' until you reach 'One thousand ten.' At that point, take your right hand, place it over your left hip, and pull the rip cord. This will open your chute."

The anxious young man yelled out from the back of the line, "Captain, what if the chute doesn't open?" The captain replied, "Well son, that's known as jumping to a conclusion."

The young man was not in the mood for jokes, so the jump captain reassured, "If nothing happens, simply put your left hand over your right hip and pull the emergency rip cord. This will open, and you will float safely to the ground. When you get to the jump site, there will be trucks to take you back to the camp. Now everyone stand and prepare to jump."

The young man was terrified, his knees were shaking, and his palms were wet. The jump captain stood looking out the door, and he suddenly yelled out, "Jump! Jump! Jump!" Everyone began to file out the door one right after another. The nervous young man was the last one in line. As the door kept getting closer and closer to him, he reluctantly continued to move forward. The jump captain kept yelling at the men, "Jump! Jump! Jump!" Finally, the young man came to the door, but he stopped dead in his tracks. Without hesitation, the jump master used his foot and booted the young man out the door.

The terrified jumper never even got out "One thousand one." He immediately put his right hand over his left hip and pulled the rip cord—nothing happened. Posthaste, he put his left hand over his right hip and pulled the emergency rip cord. Again, nothing happened. And one of his friends heard the young man say as he whizzed by, "Yep! And I bet those trucks won't be there to take me back to camp either!"

◆◆◆◆◆◆

P

141. Pastoral Call

The preacher's daughter was in bed sick with a very bad stomachache. The evening was getting late, and the little girl missed having her special play time with her father. She called down to her mother, "Mommy, could you send Daddy upstairs so I can see him." "No, dear," replied Mother, "Daddy's busy right now, and it's getting late. Go back to bed."

"But Mommy, I want to see him."

Again the mother replied, "I said, 'No!' That's enough. Go back to bed!"

"Mommy!" she said, "I'm a very sick woman, and I must see my pastor!"

❖❖❖❖❖❖

142. Patience

Little Michael came home from school with two black eyes, torn clothes, scratches, and bruises. His mother was shocked at the first sight of him, and she checked him from head to toe making sure that he was okay. Assured that little Michael was going to survive, she scolded him for getting into a fight. "I thought I taught you that when you became angry that you should count to one hundred before you made any decisions or physical responses!"

"But I did," said Michael, "the only problem is that the other boy's mother told him to count only to fifty!"

❖❖❖❖❖❖

143. Persistence

Eddie, a young lad of seven, greatly desired to have a wrist watch of his own, but his dad was reluctant to get him one. Eddie continually requested it even though his dad tenaciously refused. After several days of Eddie's repetition of, "I want a watch, I want a watch, I want a watch," etc., Dad became annoyed with Eddie's stubbornness. Finally Dad said, "Eddie, I'm tired of your continued asking for a watch. I don't want to hear another thing about it!"

That night, as was the daily custom, the family gathered in the living room for a spiritual devotion just before bedtime. Among other things, Dad would have each family member read a verse of Scripture which he or she had selected during the day. As it came Eddie's turn, he confidently announced his text saying, "My verse is Mark 13:37 where even Jesus Himself said, 'And what I say unto you I say unto all, Watch.'" (His dad got him one the next day.)

✦✦✦✦✦✦

144. Perspective

A cute little girl was sitting on the lap of her father, and she looked into a mirror at the both of them. The little girl stared at her daddy, who by all rights and excuses, was less than handsome. She looked for a long time and then asked,

Girl: Daddy? Did God make you?
Daddy: Why, yes Honey. He surely did.
Girl: And, did He make me too?
Daddy: Yes, Precious, He did that too! Why do you ask?
Girl: Oh, I was just noticing that He's doing better work these days.

✦✦✦✦✦✦

145. Perverse Parakeet

A pet shop owner had a talking parakeet for sale in his shop that had been owned by a man of lesser morals. This man had taught the parakeet to speak, and the words he spoke were less than wholesome.

One day, a lady came into his shop looking for a talking bird. The owner showed her the bird but explained the problem of this fowl's "foul" mouth. The lady completely understood the problem but related to the owner that she would like the bird and that she could cure him of this problem.

She took the bird home and talked to it about speaking only good words. The bird seemed to understand, and he did fairly well the first day. Close to the end of the second day, the parakeet blurted out a word that should not have spoken. The woman took the bird and for punishment put him in the freezer for a few minutes.

After she removed him, she said, "Do you think you can do better now and not say any bad words?" The shivering parakeet replied, "Brrrrr. Oooooo. That's cold. I'll do better, I promise."

Things went well for a few days, but unfortunately for the perverse parakeet, he slipped and once again spouted out an obscenity in the presence of some friends who were visiting the lady of the house. The woman once again got the bird and put him in the freezer. After some time when the lady's friends had left, she remembered the bird in the freezer. She had left him in there longer than she intended. Rushing to the freezer, she retrieved the bird which by this time was alive but almost stiff.

She asked the bird, "After this, do you think that you can go without a 'foul' mouth?" The bird answered with his beak chattering from the cold, "Y-Y-Yes, Mam! B-B-B-But th-th-there's one th-thing I-I-I have to kn-kn-know. Wh-Wh-What d-did that Tur-Turkey in there do?"

✦✦✦✦✦✦

146. Pig Toes

In a very small agricultural town, some farmers from the community had gotten together in order to discuss the raising of hogs and hog prices. After about thirty minutes of discussion, a woman stood up and began to give her opinions. This was a problem for one of the farmers, so he interrupted the woman, "I don't think this woman knows enough about hog farming to even speak with intelligence on the issues before us. Lady, if you know so much, tell us, how many toes does a pig have?"

The woman forthrightly replied, "You're right; I never knew that, but I have a willingness to learn. If you'll just take off your boots, I'll be glad to come and count them."

✦✦✦✦✦✦

147. Piggish Behavior

A city-dwelling family took some days of vacation to visit relatives out on the farm. They had a great time, but the only parts of the visit they really did not enjoy were the smell and squeals of the pigs.

After a year's time, the family once again wanted to visit the farm, but the father called ahead to make sure everything was okay. Unable to control himself, the father asked, "Tell me, do you still have pigs on the farm?" The reply came back, "Oh, no! We've had no pigs on the farm since you were last here."

✦✦✦✦✦✦

148. Politeness

Craig, a young man of seven, had been taught by his mother to be polite, especially when visiting other people's homes. On one such occasion, Craig had been invited to have supper with one of his friends who lived right down the street. Mother took the little man aside and once again went over the rules of politeness when visiting in the home of another. He was to remember terms like "please," "thank you," and "excuse me." Also, he was supposed to be accommodating to whatever the host and hostess say, to find something to compliment, and to be helpful and not a bother.

While the neighbor family and Craig were sitting at supper, the lady of the house asked, "Craig, are you sure that you can cut your meat okay?" Trying to be congenial in his response, he said, "Oh, yes, thank you very much. We very often have meat as tough as this at home!"

✦✦✦✦✦✦

149. Plenty for Everyone

A young boy came home from Sunday school and church, and he began to empty his pockets of pennies, nickels, dimes, and a few dollar bills. His father asked him, "Johnny, where did you get all that money?" "At church Dad," the boy replied, "they pass two plates full of it to everyone in the congregation!"

✦✦✦✦✦✦

150. Practice Makes Perfect

Buddy was not a very bright young man, and his schoolmates enjoyed making fun of him and picking on him. On one Saturday, they showed Buddy an enormous watermelon. They bet him $5.00 that he could not eat the monstrosity all at one sitting. Before he would agree, he said that he must go home for a few minutes. The schoolmates agreed, and waited for Buddy to return.

In about fifteen minutes, Buddy returned whereupon he immediately took them up on their bet. He began devouring the melon without stopping, and in just a few minutes, nothing was left of the melon but a pile of seeds and rind. The schoolmates, in shock, paid Buddy his $5.00 but asked him, "We never thought you could do it, but why did you go home just before eating the melon?"

Buddy answered as he wiped the juice from his mouth, "Mother had a bigger melon than this at home, and I figured if I could eat the bigger one, then I would have no trouble in eating this smaller one!"

✦✦✦✦✦✦

151. Praise the Lord

Back in the days of circuit-riding preachers, an evangelist was in need of a new horse. He went to an auction, and some of his friends put him on to a good deal for a horse that would suit him perfectly. They explained how the horse had been trained to respond by different commands than other horses. Instead of "Giddy Up," this horse started by the rider saying, "Praise the Lord," and instead of "Whoa," this horse stopped through the use of the word "Amen." What a novelty for the evangelist, so he bought the horse immediately.

He got up on the horse and said, "Praise the Lord." Straightway, the horse trotted off down the trail. After traveling a short distance, the evangelist pulled out the Scriptures and began to read while letting the horse continue down the trail. All of a sudden, the preacher looked up and saw they were coming to the edge of a cliff. The preacher screamed out in fear, "Whoa! Whoa! Stop!" Then at the last moment, at the very edge of the cliff, he remembered the right command. He said, "Amen!"

The horse stopped dead in his tracks. The preacher took off his hat and wiped the sweat that appeared over his brow. In thankfulness, he said, "Praise the Lord!"

✦✦✦✦✦✦

152. Preacher's Notes

Preachers fall into four main categories in relation to their use of sermon notes, that is, from the congregations's viewpoint.

One: Preachers who never use notes, and therefore, the congregation never knows how close they are to finishing their sermons.

Two: Preachers who have their sermons on paper in front of them on the podium and who conspicuously place their pages on the side of the podium so the congregation can know how much longer they will speak gauged by the amount of pages left.

Three: Preachers who have notes on paper but confuse the congregation by putting the first and succeeding pages on the back of the stack from which they are using, and, thus, the congregation never knows when the end is coming.

Four: Preachers who place their sermons on paper, who place each sheet on the side of the podium as they preach, but after placing the last sheet on the side, horrify the congregation by picking up the whole stack and begin reading from the backside.

153. Preparation for Life

A woman had lived a good life; however, she had faced some hard times. At this particular day, she stood over the recent grave of her fourth husband. For many reasons she was sad, but she began to reminisce about the long life she had lived. As she looked over the cemetery, she noticed all the grave sites for each of her husbands. Her mind went back to each one and how each had contributed significantly to her present state of life.

She thought of her first husband: a banker. They had married young in life and were very content with each other. It was during this time in her life that she gained financial security through her husband's ability in money matters. She became a prominent figure in the city and was well respected as a philanthropist with a heart. When this husband died, he left her well endowed with life insurance provisions and with his personal inheritance.

She thought of her second husband: an actor. For some years she had followed the career of this man who was passionate for the stage. His performances were moving experiences, and the woman took every opportunity to see him perform. Later they got married, and she followed him as he performed all over the world, for she could not get enough of his acting. However, after a few years, he died.

She thought of her third husband: a minister. In trying to resolve the sadness in her life, she went to church finally finding solace more than she thought possible. She and the minister fell in love and were married. It was during this time of her life that she made spiritual preparations for the life to come and made sure that her relationship with God was right. She greatly enjoyed her life and the joy she now knew. Unfortunately, after some time, the minister passed away also.

She thought of her most recent husband, the fourth: a funeral director. After so many visits to the funeral home, she became well accustomed to seeing this caring man. With the passing of time, she felt so comfortable around him. Their relationship blossomed until the moment came when they got married. Their life together was quite enjoyable, relaxed, and comforting. It was during this time in her life that her husband helped her make preparations for her own physical death. She made all the arrangements necessary for her eventual burial needs. Unfortunately, the funeral director died.

As the widow now looked over the cemetery, seeing all four of the grave stones of her former husbands, her life racing before her, in that moment she realized how each husband had contributed to her life. For in that she had married a banker, an actor, a minister, and a funeral director, she immediately realized that she had married "One for the money," "Two for the show," "Three to get ready," and "Four to go."

154. Preparation for the After-Life

A Russian gentleman was sitting on the curb side in Moscow engrossed in deep study. Everyone who passed could easily see that the man was intense in his mental research. A policeman coming by, became inquisitive, so he asked, "Tell me sir, what are you studying so seriously?"

"Oh," he said, "I am studying the Hebrew language."

"Why is studying Hebrew so important to you?" the policeman asked.

"Well, it is like this, I expect to go to Heaven, and once I get there I want to speak to God in His own language, Hebrew!"

"But after all this work and labor you are going through, what if you end up in hell?"

"Well," he answered, "in that case, Russian I already know!"

✦✦✦✦✦✦

155. Prideful Approach

A preacher had become known for his great oratory, homiletical insight, and tremendous use of language, and he was invited to speak at a large convention in front of thousands of people. Proud of his abilities and beginning to rest on the laurels from the past, he strutted himself to the pulpit for the main convention sermon. He had not given this sermon his usual level of concentration, prayer, or study; however, he was sure of calling upon his own power of excellence to once again gain the accolades of the listeners.

As he began to preach, he realized that the message had no power or impact. He called upon every preaching aid he could think of while he spoke there, but with every effort came more crushing public defeat. He could notice that the sermon was dead and that the people were bored and uninterested. After he concluded the sermon, he went back to his motel room in the throes of despondency and dejection. As he sat on the edge of the bed with his head hung in humility, his wife said, "Honey, if you had gone to the pulpit the way you just came down, then you could have come down the way you went up!"

✦✦✦✦✦✦

156. Profanity

The pastor and one of his deacons went to the Country Club to play golf. They were both doing fairly well until the ninth hole. The pastor teed up, addressed the ball, made a beautiful and powerful swing at the ball; however, the ball tumbled off the tee, traveling only about six feet instead of the pastor's usual straight and powerful fairway drive.

The pastor stood there glaring at the ball resting just beyond where he stood, but he never spoke nor breathed a word. After just a moment of observation, the deacon said, "Pastor, that is the most profane silence I believe I have ever heard!"

✦✦✦✦✦✦

157. Profiting from Evil

At the conclusion of the morning worship hour, a man spoke with his pastor about the morning message.

Man: Pastor, I found your morning message to be quite intriguing and thought provoking.
Pastor: Why, thank you so much. What was it that so caught your deeper contemplation?
Man: It was the part where you said it was wrong to profit from evil.
Pastor: Yes, this is so true.
Man: Also, I was convicted about your saying how wrong it was for someone else to profit from another man's sin.
Pastor: Yes, this is true also.
Man: But Pastor, do you really believe this applies to all our lives today, to all of us?
Pastor: Quite honestly, I do. Why do you ask?
Man: I'd like for you to return the fifty dollars I gave you last year for marrying me.

✦✦✦✦✦✦

158. Promise of Better

A pastor at a church for six years had resigned and was making his move to another city. He held his last service in his old church, and in his honor, the congregation had provided a very nice "going-away" fellowship. As the pastor made his way around the room, one older lady began weeping almost uncontrollably. The pastor, trying to comfort and console her, said, "Sister, I am sure that after I am gone, someone even better than myself will come and be your pastor." The lady broke out crying even more, forcing these words through her tears, "But that's what we were told the last two times."

159. Proper Protocol

An inexperienced soldier was stationed as sentry at his military post. His instructions were quite clear; he was to let no one pass the gate unless the car had a post sticker on the windshield. His night had been rather uneventful until a large car came to the gate. The chauffeur was a corporal and in the back seat was a general; however, there was no sticker on the car.

The sentry said, "Halt, who goes there?"

The corporal rolled down the window and replied, "I am a corporal, and this is General Peterson. Open the gate."

"I'm sorry, sir," the private replied, "I have orders that no one is to enter this gate without the proper vehicle identification."

The general spoke from the back seat, "Drive on, corporal." The sentry protested again, "Sir, I have orders to shoot anyone who drives through without authorization."

The general once again demanded, "This is ridiculous. Drive on, Corporal." The private came to the window and enquired, "Excuse me, General, but I'm new at this. As you go by, whom do I shoot? You or the corporal?"

✦✦✦✦✦✦

160. Protesting

A young social idealist spoke to his girl friend, "I'm going over to the college office to make sure that my Federal Education Grant is still going to be sent, and then I'll stop by the Welfare office to pick up our food stamps. I'll also go by and see if my unemployment check has arrived for this week. While I'm doing that, why don't you go on by the county Free Health Clinic for the check-up you've been needing. That will give us enough time to meet at the Federal building downtown this afternoon so that we can join the protest against governmental overspending!"

✦✦✦✦✦✦

161. Prunes

Bobby was a young lad of nine who had grown up in a home with very strict Christian values. His parents had taught him to be very good, to work hard at school, and to do his chores. An obedient young man, Bobby had made his parents proud by his obedience and good spirit; however, for whatever reason, Bobby came to breakfast one morning in a very disagreeable mood. His mother had some prunes on his plate, but Bobby refused straightforwardly yelling, "I don't want prunes, and I'm not going to eat them either!"

Both parents were astonished at his reaction, and his father said, "Bobby, you know in your heart and mind that God has commanded children to honor and obey their parents. You also know that God will punish children who do not. We and the Lord want you to eat these prunes." The little man defiantly refused. The parents put the prunes in the refrigerator, and for correction, sent Bobby back to his room until he should come down and eat the detestable fruit. He indignantly retreated to the bedroom.

In only a few minutes, a dreadful thunderstorm came up with flashes of lightning and boisterous claps of thunder all around the house. The parents said to themselves, "This is perfect timing. Maybe this will teach Bobby a lesson." During the continued storm, Bobby came down to the kitchen and opened the refrigerator. Another flash of lightning hit nearby and the thunder shook the house. Mom and Dad could hear Bobby's comment from the kitchen as he ate a prune, "Man! What a big fuss over a few prunes!"

◆◆◆◆◆◆

R

162. Repetition

Dr. Sanderson had several new lists of vocabulary words prepared for his college freshman English class. Wanting to get the students to learn them but also to encourage their use, he taught the students that repetition would be helpful in the retaining of information. He went on to say, "If you will repeat a word fifteen or twenty times, I guarantee that it will become yours for the rest of life."

From the back of the class, Jill closed her eyes and began to speak to herself in soft, determined tones, "Billy, Billy, Billy . . . ."

✦✦✦✦✦✦

163. Respect is in the Eye of the Beholder

The capital of Sudan, Khartoum, is on the banks of the Nile. Housed there is Gordon College which was named after the famous British General Charles Gordon (1833-1885), killed in battle at Khartoum in 1885. In the college gardens, a magnificent statue was erected of General Gordon sitting on a camel. The general is in full military dress, and the camel appears in a grand array of tapestries.

For many years, a British native worked in Khartoum, and he would often take his young son to see the impressive statue and to admire the general. The father and son would stand side by side looking at the stately figure. However, the Englishman was being transferred to another field position, so he decided to take his son to the statue of Gordon for the last time.

They both stood there silently, the father wiping a tear from his eye. As they turned to leave, the boy looked up at his father and asked, "Father? I have always wondered about something. Who is that funny-looking man sitting on Gordon?"

✦✦✦✦✦✦

164. Right Answer

The pastor of the church was taking a special but brief time during the Sunday evening service to speak to the children. Each Sunday evening, he would teach them different lessons, many about Jesus and how important He was to their lives. In one lesson, the pastor had a particular illustration in mind, and so, he posed a riddle to the youngsters.

He asked, "What is it that lives in the woods, collects nuts for winter, climbs trees, and has a bushy tail?"

A bright young lad blurted out in front of the whole congregation, "I know the answer is supposed to be Jesus, but it sure sounds like a squirrel to me!"

✦✦✦✦✦✦

165. Right Change

Two city slickers were driving through the country, speaking to one another how dumb they thought country folk were. Not able to contain themselves any longer, they thought of a trick to pull on some unsuspecting farmer. Soon they drove by an old farmer alongside his run-down shack. They pulled up in their shiny new car and called out to the farmer, "Hey, Farmer Joe, can you change an eighteen-dollar bill?" The farmer nodded and slowly said, "Sure, but I gotta go inside and get some money." He went inside.

With the farmer gone, the two slickers took a ten dollar bill and marked the zero to look like an eight. "He'll never know the difference," they said to each other.

The farmer soon returned with a worn and tattered wallet. He took the bill from the city men and looked it over carefully. Tucking it away safely in his pocket, the farmer pulled out one-dollar bills that he had clearly marked over. He grinned at the young men as he replied, "How do you want the change? Two nines or three sixes?"

✦✦✦✦✦✦

166. Righteous Indignation

It was in the middle of the night inside the modest home of a Quaker. In the stillness of those night hours, the lady of the house whispered to her husband, "Didst thou not hear that noise which camest from the kitchen?"

The husband arose from his bed quietly and retrieved his shotgun. He slowly made his way to the kitchen where he saw the midnight intruder, robbing them of their silverware. The Quaker aimed his trusty weapon in the direction of the robber and so gently spoke, "Dear Friend, I certainly do mean thee no harm nor hurt; yet, thou standest where I expecteth to shoot."

✦✦✦✦✦✦

Humorous Stories

167. Rmmmbumbum

A city slicker bought a new tract of land in the country on which he wanted to build his family dream home. Because he desired to "get back to nature," he decided to clear the land himself. He went to a local hardware store to buy a chain saw. The clerk showed him several models, but one model the clerk guaranteed would cut through fifteen trees a day. The city man bought it and went off to the work of clearing trees.

After about a week, the slicker came back to the hardware store quite angry and complaining that the clerk had sold him a faulty chain saw. He spouted off, "Instead of fifteen trees, the best I can get from it is three trees a day." The clerk took the saw in hand, pulled the cord, and the machine immediately fired up going, "Rmmmbumbum, Rmmmbumbum, Rmmmbumbum." The city slicker gasped in surprise, "What? What's that noise?"

✦✦✦✦✦✦

168. Rudolph

Tony and Alicia were traveling through Russia with an experienced, native tour guide named Rudolph. The guide showed them some of the most spectacular sites in Russia, but Tony always questioned the details given by the guide. In fact, there came to be a growing tension between Rudolph and Tony about every subject.

Nearing their end of travels in Moscow, Tony looked out from the van window and commented, "Oh, look Alicia, it's snowing!"

Immediately, Rudolph responded, "I am sorry sir, this is not snow; it's merely rain."

"I'm telling you, that is snow out there!" Tony argued.

Alicia quickly broke in the argument saying to Tony, "I do believe that Rudolph, the Red, knows rain, dear."

✦✦✦✦✦✦

S

169. Seeking a Sign

A pastor had just put out a new and expensive announcement sign in front of the church, which was immediately stolen and hidden by the mischievous teenagers of the church. Searching for the sign several days, the pastor finally found it but hid it elsewhere.

He had a meeting with the teens after the Wednesday evening service, informing them that unless the sign was returned by that Saturday night, they would forfeit their church activities for the remainder of the year. The teens searched diligently but never found the sign.

That Sunday morning, the pastor appeared before the congregation and the distressed teenagers. He read his morning text: "A wicked and adulterous generation seeketh for a sign and there shall be none given unto them."

✦✦✦✦✦✦

170. Self-Control

Just outside the back door of a city butcher shop, two flies found some bologna on the sidewalk. It had been in the hot sun, and it was just right for their enjoyment. They both "flew" on the feast of meat until one of them had eaten all its little body could hold. This one flew up and landed on a nearby broom handle that was leaning beside the door.

The other fly kept eating and eating and eating. He ate so much that the first fly was more than a little embarrassed to see the gluttony of his friend. Finally, the second fly stopped eating and began to fly up to his friend, but he had eaten so much it took all his strength to make it up on the broom handle. Both flies began to converse.

Fly one:	I am terribly ashamed of you and how gluttonous you are.
Fly two:	Maybe so, but wow, was that ever good.
Fly one:	It was good, but you should begin to show more self control. You were so weighted down, you hardly made it to this broom handle.
Fly two:	(Looking at the remaining bologna below.) You know, that food still looks good. In fact, the more I look at it, the hungrier I get.
Fly one:	You can hardly fly as it is! How can you pack yourself with more?
Fly two:	I don't know about that, but I've got to have more.

Preparing himself carefully, the second fly buzzed off from the broom, but he didn't have the strength and stamina to continue his flight. He rocketed downward falling to his death in a splat on the concrete.

The moral of the story? "Don't fly off the handle if you're full of bologna."

✦✦✦✦✦✦

171. Sermon Assessment

A visiting evangelist had begun a week's meeting at a church with the first service on a Sunday morning. The church, to encourage a large attendance for the first service, had planned a meal immediately after the morning service. The attendance was good as well as the food for the fellowship meal. While everyone was finishing the meal, the evangelist was making his way around the crowd, trying to make acquaintance with each person.

As he did so, one particular and peculiar man came to the evangelist, looked him square in the eye, and said, "Sermon's too long." The strange man immediately walked away into the crowd. The evangelist thought that it was strange, but he brushed off the comment as he continued talking to people. Not long after, the peculiar man once again approached the evangelist and said, "Sermon's too loud." The man walked away quickly with no other comment. This time the evangelist had more difficulty throwing off the statement.

It was not long before the stranger once again approached the evangelist and said, "Sermon's boring." At this point, the visiting speaker could take it no longer, so he pulled the pastor aside to find out about this unusual man.

He explained to the pastor how the man would come to him, make a short statement, and immediately walk away. The pastor laughed saying, "Oh, don't pay him any mind. He only repeats what he hears!"

✦✦✦✦✦✦

172. Shorter Sermon 1

The pastor of the local church was known for his long sermons, and the congregation wished for some tactful means of letting him know that they would like the messages to be a little more brief. On one particular Sunday, the pastor came to the church with one of his fingers wrapped in a rather large bandage. The chairman of the deacon board asked, "Pastor, what happened to you? How did you hurt your finger?"

The pastor answered, "I'm a little embarrassed because I was thinking about my sermon for today, and I cut my finger."

"Well," replied the deacon, "next time I suggest that you think more about your finger and cut your sermon instead."

✦✦✦✦✦✦

173. Shorter Sermon 2

Over the passing months, the pastor of the local church gradually made his sermons longer and longer. In fact, his messages were getting so long that the congregation was more than a little bothered. Many of the members talked to the deacon board expressing that they loved their pastor but also requesting that something be done. At the next deacon's meeting, the chairman of the board approached the pastor concerning the matter.

"Don't you understand," the pastor replied, "I am giving you and the congregation the milk of the Word?"

"Of course, Pastor," responded the chairman, "but what we are requesting is that you give us condensed milk!"

✦✦✦✦✦✦

174. Sermon Sleeping

A man in the congregation was faithful in attending church, but he was also faithful in sleeping through every service. No sooner did a service begin before the man would doze off. Because this had become an embarrassment to his wife, she counseled with friends about how to stop this unwanted behavior. One friend suggested that she get some high-smelling Limburger cheese, put it a zip-lock bag, and place it in her purse for just the proper moment during the service.

The wife did as directed, and at the next Sunday service, her husband faithfully began to nod. She took the cheese from her purse, opened the zip-lock bag right under his nose for him to get a big whiff. All of a sudden, his head drew back from the smell, and he said, "No, Nancy, no—don't kiss me now, Nancy!"

✦✦✦✦✦✦

175. Sin of Pride

A lady came to the pastor's office to counsel with him concerning a particular sin in her life.

Lady: Pastor, I have a terrible sin that I need to confess, and I need some help in overcoming it in the future.
Pastor: Well, yes, tell me about it.
Lady: You see, Pastor, I cannot resist the temptation of sitting in front of my mirror, most days as much as four or five hours.
Pastor: What is that you are doing there so long?
Lady: My sin is ... ah ... well ... that I sit there to admire my great beauty.
Pastor: Oh, sister, you have nothing to worry about. There's no sin of pride here. You just have an over-active imagination!

✦✦✦✦✦✦

176. Sin Will Find You Out

A lady came into the shop of the neighborhood butcher requesting to buy a chicken. The butcher went to the freezer noticing that he had only one fryer left. He brought it over to the scales and weighed it. "Miss, this is a good hen; that'll be $3.99."

The lady hesitated and then said, "Well, I'm not sure that this one will be enough. I really needed a larger bird."

"Why sure, Mam," replied the butcher as he replaced the bird in the freezer. He rolled the frozen fowl around of couple of times in the ice and returned to the scales with the same bird. He weighed it again, placing his thumb on the scale.

"How's that Mam? That'll be $4.67."

"Oh, that's great," she said, "I'll take them both!"

✦✦✦✦✦✦

177. Sorry You're Gone

A man, weeping uncontrollably, had thrown himself over a grave. As he cried, he spoke these endearing words, "Oh, why did you have to die? Life has never been the same since you left; life has now lost its meaning for me, and its joy is gone. If fate had not taken you away, if only you were still here, everything would be different. Why did you die, oh why did you have to die?"

A passerby heard the extreme grief expressed by the man, and he came by to pay his condolences and to see if he might bring any comfort. The passerby said, "I'm so sorry, friend. I can tell you have faced a great loss. Tell me, who is this person for whom you grieve so much? I am sure it was someone of great importance."

"Importance?" replied the griever, "You can't even imagine how important. It was my wife's first husband!"

178. Speaker of Rank

For the evangelistic meeting planned for the church, the pastor was attempting to think of various introductions for variety in presenting the visiting evangelist to the congregation. On the first night, the pastor wanted to communicate just how important a man had come to speak to them. He began, "Dear friends, many men of reputation and distinction have come to speak to us on previous occasions. We have indeed been privileged. Although we are thankful for the great men of rank who have spoken here before, I want you to welcome Evangelist Bladen, the rankest of them all."

✦✦✦✦✦✦

179. Special Delivery

John, a young man who was not the brightest in the world, got a new job as a delivery boy for a local pet shop. One of his first deliveries was a rabbit which he was supposed to take to a lady named Mrs. Woodard at 1234 Forest Lane. John wrote the name and address on a piece of paper just to make sure that he would not forget. He got the rabbit, placed him in a cage, placed it in his truck, and off he went.

Every couple of minutes, John would have to look at the paper in his shirt pocket, just to remember where he was going. He would repeat it to himself, "Mrs. Woodard at 1234 Forest Lane, Mrs. Woodard at 1234 Forest Lane." While looking at his slip of paper, he hit a huge pothole, and his truck swerved off the road and into the ditch. The commotion of the small accident caused the door of the rabbit cage to fly open, and the rabbit hopped for its little life across the open field and into the woods.

John, seeing what had happened, watched to see what direction the rabbit was going. He pulled out the slip of paper from his pocket, looked at the address, and began laughing uncontrollably. A passer-by saw John laughing, and asked what was so funny. John replied, "That dumb old rabbit just ran across the field and into the woods over yonder. He'll never find where he's supposed to go because I have the address right here in my pocket!"

✦✦✦✦✦✦

180. Spiritual Excitement

Wayne had taken a few days off from work in order to attend a three-day college Bible conference. The services were excellent with spirited singing, powerful preaching, and enjoyable fellowship. When he returned home, Wayne could hardly contain his excitement about what had taken place and the difference it had made in his life in just a short time. He beamed about it everywhere he went.

He was still in that state of being when he went to church the following Sunday. The pastor, sensing that Wayne had realized some spiritual victories in his life, asked him to lead in prayer. Wayne immediately began with a prayer of thanksgiving, saying, "Dear Lord, the conference this week was the most inspirational meeting in which I've ever been. The close fellowship of the saints was so comforting. The music was encouraging to the soul. And the preaching, oh, the preaching was so dynamic and moving! How can I even find the words to explain it? Oh Lord—you just should have been there yourself to witness it!"

✦✦✦✦✦✦

181.   Standing in the Need of Prayer

A family had come to Washington, D.C., to tour the Capitol grounds. As they entered the legislative rooms, they noticed a quite handsome, distinguished gentleman standing in the wings. They enquired of their guide who this man was. He said, "That gentleman is the chaplain."

"Does he stand at the podium and pray for the Senate and the House?" they asked.

"No, not exactly," replied the guide. "He comes to the podium, looks at our legislators and then earnestly prays for the country."

✦✦✦✦✦✦

182.   Success Oriented

Two very experienced fishermen had acquired all the equipment and knowledge to perform exceptionally well at fishing, and they especially enjoyed ice fishing. On one such ice-fishing trip, they selected a good spot and drilled holes in the ice about twenty-five feet apart. They put worms on their hooks, dropped the lines in the water; however, even after fishing several hours, they still had not gotten even the slightest nibble.

About mid-day, a young boy came out on the ice, cut a hole between the two men, baited his hook, and began fishing too. He had no more put his hook in the water when he pulled up a nice fish. After re-baiting, he caught another and another and another. The two experienced fishermen were flabbergasted. Finally, one of the men came to the young boy and asked, "Tell me, young fellow, what is your secret for catching fish?"

The boy replied, "Mmmm yymm mmmms wmmm."

"What did you say?" the man asked.

Again the boy said, "Mmmm yymm mmmms wmmm."

"I'm sorry, young man, but I can't understand a word you're saying. Could you please speak a little more clearly!"

The boy cupped his hands, spit out a large mass from his mouth, and said, "Keep your worms warm!"

✦✦✦✦✦✦

183. Successful Marriage

A couple had been married for fifteen years, and everyone noted how successful their marriage appeared to be. At a gathering of friends, this topic once again came to light as the item of discussion. The group finally cornered the couple and asked for them to give the secret of their apparent success.

The couple embarrassingly looked at each other, and then the husband said, "Well folks, it's truly like this. The secret to our marriage success is that since long ago we spend quality time at a restaurant with great atmosphere at least two times each week. There we enjoy a meal by candlelight, soothing music, a wonderful dinner, and a quiet walk home in the moonlight. She goes on Tuesdays, and I go on Fridays."

✦✦✦✦✦✦

184. Surprise Visit

A pastor had made it a practice to make consistent visits yearly into the homes of his church members. One particular family, although not especially well to do, made every public pretense of high living and high moral standards. On one occasion, the pastor arrived for a prearranged afternoon visit with the family, and he was invited to the parlor for refreshments. The room was decorated beautifully; tea, coffee, and cake were provided; and all were at their best behavior. The pastor remarked to the family, "I'm so glad to see that you are housed so comfortably and living so devoutly." The little girl in the family spoke up, "Oh, preacher, if you want to know how we really live, you need to come when you're not here!"

✦✦✦✦✦✦

185. Swallow Hard

A man came to his doctor complaining about a sore foot. He limped from the car, into the waiting room, and back to the examination room. The doctor and nurse came into the room, and after a brief observation, the doctor handed the man a rather massive-sized pill. The nurse began asking the doctor some questions concerning treatment, so the man hobbled over to the sink and forced down the pill.

As he got back to the table, the doctor said, "Okay, now drop that pill in this bucket of water, and we'll soak your foot."

✦✦✦✦✦✦

186. Swiping Swill

The chief editors of two city newspapers were constantly at one another's literary throats. The contention got so bad that both used their editorial pages to take "swipes" at each other.

One day, the editor for the Daily Gazette wrote in his editorial, "The editor of Today's Journal is so mean and low down that he would steal the swill from a putrid pig!"

In the next day's issue, the editor of Today's Journal replied in his editorial, "The editor of the Daily Gazette knows full well I never stole his swill."

✦✦✦✦✦✦

T

187. Tabloid Headlines

A man who owned an infamous tabloid newspaper was getting ready to retire, but he did not know which of his three sons he would have to head the company upon his retirement. In order to resolve the matter, he proposed a contest between his sons. He brought them into his office and told them the following conditions. "My sons, I will select from the three of you, one to be the head of the newspaper. I have a contest for you, and the one who wins will head the paper. I will select the one who writes the most sensational headline in only three words. Report back to me tomorrow morning with the headlines." The three sons departed to their respective offices and began to write. The next morning, the sons arrived at their father's office as required.

The first son's headline reported, "Castro Rejects Communism."

The second son revealed this headline, "Saddam Becomes Christian."

Hands down, the third son inherited the newspaper's presidency when he presented his headline of three words, "The Pope Elopes."

✦✦✦✦✦✦

188. Take Him at His Word

A man was having a yard sale, and posted at the dog house was a sign that read, "Talking Dog for Sale—$5.00." An inquisitive buyer asked about the dog and said to the owner, "Now you have to know that there is no such thing as a talking dog. This is impossible!"

In reply, the dog bounded from his house jumping up on the buyer, "Please, kind sir, please buy me. This man is cruel, he never feeds me, never gives me a bath, and never takes me for walks. I have traveled the world over and been one of the richest dog acts ever. I have played before presidents, heads of state, and royalty. I promise to give you a good life, but please, please, please buy me!"

In shock, the buyer said to the seller, "That's amazing! He can talk just like you said. But what on earth could ever make you sell him for only $5.00?"

"Because," he said, "I'm sick and tired of all his lies!"

✦✦✦✦✦✦

189. Telemarketing

A telemarketer was calling through the phone list when he made contact with a four-year old boy. The conversation went like this:

Salesman: Hello. Is your mother there?
Boy: Yes, but she can't come to the phone right now.
Salesman: Okay. Is your father there, so that I may speak with him?
Boy: No. He's not here right now.
Salesman: Well, is there anyone else there?
Boy: Yes. My sister is here.
Salesman: That's good. Would you get her please?
Boy: I guess I could.

A long silence came until the little boy once again returned to the phone.

Boy: Hello?
Salesman: Yes. It's you again, isn't it? I thought you were going to get your sister.
Boy: I did, but I can't get her out of the crib.

✦✦✦✦✦✦

190. Telling the Truth

Three local pastors enjoyed getting together every Monday morning at a local restaurant for breakfast. They enjoyed the fellowship together and the encouragement they felt by discussing and helping one another resolve problems encountered in the ministry. On one Monday morning, they discussed the Scriptural command of James 5:16, "Confess your faults one to another...." All three, realizing that they had weaknesses, pledged to acknowledge their greatest faults—yes, their own secret sins—to the others in the group.

Pastor 1: I must admit to you that I have a problem with stealing. I know it's terrible, but when the offering plates are put in my office, and when no one is looking, I take a couple of ten dollar bills and stick them in my pocket. The temptation is just too great for me. I can hardly help myself.

Pastor 2: Well, my greatest sin is that I will often times lie about things to make myself look better in the eyes of others. I have had a problem with this for many years, and what a difference it is for me to be so honest and straightforward today.

Pastor 3: Men, I think my sin is the worst of them all. It is a sin that I have never gotten the victory over in all these years. My greatest sin is that of gossip! And, oh, I can't wait to get out of here today!

191. Terminal Case

A couple had been married for about twenty-five years when the husband acquired acute symptoms of a terminal illness. The man went through days of intense testing to discover the cause of his deteriorating condition. After the last battery of tests, the man was sent back to his hospital room, and the doctor arrived in the waiting room to speak to the man's wife.

The doctor began, "Madam, we've given your husband every test imaginable, and my colleagues and I all agree that the only way your husband can avoid death is to receive tender loving care, to be waited on, to have his meals served to him in bed, and to be given peace and contentment at home." With a tear in her eye, she thanked the doctor for all he had done.

She returned to her husband's room. He soon awoke and asked his wife about the doctor's diagnosis. She replied without hesitancy, "I'm so sorry, Honey. He said you were going to die."

✦✦✦✦✦✦

192. Thankful for What You Get

A lawyer had been employed by a wealthy business man to defend him in an important court case. He did a wonderful job winning the case for his client. The business man, in a spirit of appreciation, took the lawyer to one of the most prestigious restaurants in town. At the conclusion of the meal, the business man spoke of his sincere appreciation for the job well done. As a further expression of thanks, he handed the lawyer a highly expensive, hand-crafted and detailed leather wallet.

The lawyer looked at it and became quite upset. He hastily returned the wallet and spouted off at the business man, "Look, I've worked endlessly for your defense in this recent matter. The method of payment owed me is not fancy meals or expensive gifts. For services like I've rendered to you, I would normally receive four thousand dollars."

The business man took the wallet, opened it, and looking at the money inside, removed six, crisp, one thousand dollar bills. With a smile, he returned the wallet to the lawyer saying, "Here is your required fee. Thank you for your services."

✦✦✦✦✦✦

193. That's What It Says

Jason and Jeremy, two young boys from the farm, were taking a stroll downtown. Just learning how to read a little, they were entertaining themselves reading all the signs in the store windows. Going store to store, each one would take a turn reading a sign to the other. Then, they came upon this sign.

Jason read it, "Cast Iron Sinks"

Jeremy replied, "Duh. We may be children, but even we know that!"

✦✦✦✦✦✦

194. Told You

A dinner party was being given in the home of a prominent family in town, and the children had been put to bed early so as not to disturb the guests. Just as the guests were being seated at the dinner table, the host's two children came into the room without a stitch of clothes on. As they walked through the room, they did so slowly and quietly but with no pretense of hiding themselves. The parents were so embarrassed, they payed no attention to the children and pretended that nothing was amiss. The guests followed suit and went on with the conservation as though nothing was out of the ordinary.

As the children departed the room, a hush fell on the crowd. In that moment of silence, one of the children was heard saying to the other, "See, I told you. It is vanishing cream!"

✦✦✦✦✦✦

195. Tongue Tied

A young preacher at his first church was quite nervous about having to perform any of the new ministries of which he was not yet accustomed. The Sunday was soon arriving that he would have to conduct his first baptism and communion service. In order to be ready at the appropriate time, he practiced for hours on end by memorizing exactly what to say.

The only problem he faced was that the baptismal and communion services fell on the same day and service. He tried to keep his composure as well as the memorized speeches rehearsed in his mind. As it came time for the first baptism, the young preacher got tongue tied and as he put the person under the water, he said, "And drink ye all of it."

Humorous Stories

196. Too Many Questions

A little yet spunky three-year-old named Peter had to visit the doctor for a check-up. The pediatrician, in trying to make the young man feel more comfortable, began the conversation like this:

Doctor: Well, good morning Peter!
Peter: Good morning, Doctor.
Doctor: Okay, Peter. You sit right up here on the edge of my table. I have a few questions I want to ask you.
Peter: Okay, Doctor.
Doctor: Tell me, Peter, (touching Peter's nose) is this your nose?
Peter: Yes sir.
Doctor: And Peter, (touching Peter's mouth) is this your mouth?
Peter: Yes sir.
Doctor: (Wanting to make sure that Peter really knew what he was answering, touched Peter's ear.) And now, is this your eyes?
Peter: (Turning to his mother) Mother? I think we need to look for another doctor.

✦✦✦✦✦✦

197. Truth or Pride

A local pastor, one who had always been known for his candor, was a witness in a federal court case. The first lawyer to question the pastor began by asking several background questions. The counselor asked about his occupation, and he went further to ask the preacher of his personal assessment of his pastoral abilities.

Without hesitation, the pastor said, "I am the greatest living preacher of all time."

"What?" asked the lawyer in surprise. "How can you make such a statement as bold as that?"

"Well," said the pastor, "I am under oath. I certainly don't want to commit perjury!"

✦✦✦✦✦✦

198. Turn It Off

The preacher of a sizeable and enthusiastic church was well known for his ability to handle difficult situations on the spur of the moment. On one Sunday, the preacher was waxing eloquent when his youngest son entered the main service unexpectedly and boisterously. The lad ran down the center aisle making the sounds of a racing car in view and earshot of all. "Brrrmmmmm, brrrrmmmm" came from his little mouth and "beep, beep, beep" as he began to run between the pews and the surprised congregation. His little hands were on his make believe steering wheel as he quickly made his way left and right.

The preacher stopped his sermon, pointed at his son, and demanded, "Billy, park the car immediately in the parking space beside your mother right there on that pew (he pointed). Turn off the ignition, and hand her the keys."

The sermon continued undisturbed—well, after a good laugh by the congregation.

✦✦✦✦✦✦

199.   Two-Faced

A debate was held in 1858 by Abraham Lincoln (1809-1865) and Stephen Douglas (1813-1861) for a U.S. Senate seat. Douglas was known as a great orator, where Lincoln had less ability in speaking as well as not being as comely in appearance. During the debate, Douglas charged Lincoln with being two-faced. Lincoln quickly replied, "I leave it for my audience to decide. If I had two faces, would I indeed be wearing this one?"

✦✦✦✦✦✦

U

200. Ugly

Hank: Farmer Joe have a daughter?
Frank: He sure does.
Hank: Is she pretty or ugly?
Frank: She's uglier than sin.
Hank: How ugly's that?
Frank: She's so ugly that when she stood in the cornfield, the crows thought she was a scarecrow.
Hank: That's ugly! But did she scare the crows away?
Frank: Not only that, she scared 'em so bad, they brought back the corn they'd taken three days before!

✦✦✦✦✦✦

201. Unpaid Debts

A young man had acquired some debts, but he was reluctant to be faithful in paying his bills. One particular creditor had sent notices to the young man monthly for over a year, encouraging, pleading, and even threatening him to pay his bill. Finally in frustration, the creditor sent this notice, "Your debt has been on our accounting books for over a year now. We want to remind you that we have now carried you longer than even your mother did. It's time for us to be delivered of you!"

✦✦✦✦✦✦

202. Untasty Diet Food

Father had become a little overweight and had been ordered by the doctor to go on a strict diet. Unfortunately, this also meant the rest of the family changing their eating habits also. There were no longer to be red meats, rich desserts, or junk food; all that was left to eat were the nourishing fruits, vegetables, and various types of fish. Although this was difficult for Father, Jeremy, the youngest boy, had an especially difficult time.

Mother tried to find some tasty variety in the menu; however, this was not always possible. For one meal, Mother had prepared fish and asparagus. Little

Jeremy had been laboring to get some of the food down, but he was slowly losing the battle. As he was chewing on the fish, he came across a bone. He pulled it from his mouth and asked Mother, "What am I supposed to do with this?"

Mother answered, "Just put it in a place where you are sure you won't eat it." The little boy obediently put it in the asparagus.

❖❖❖❖❖❖

203. Updated Colloquialisms

Many changes are taking place in our world, especially that of our weights and measurements going to the metric system. Yet, many of the colloquial expressions we have become accustomed to are based on standard weights and measurements. With the shift to metrics, it appears that a myriad of these idioms will have to be changed. Instead of using "miles, pounds, and yards," we will have to change to "meters, grams, liters, and kilometers." See how some of our old expressions will change:

(1) Put your best 0.3 of a meter forward.
(2) Give a man 2.5 centimeters and he'll take 1.6 kilometers.
(3) A miss is as good as 1.6 kilometers.
(4) Twenty-eight grams of prevention is worth 453 grams of cure.
(5) Peter Piper picked 8.8 liters of pickled peppers.
(6) Walk 1.6 kilometers in his shoes.

❖❖❖❖❖❖

204. Useless

During an Army war game, a commanding officer's vehicle got stuck in an off-road mud slick. Standing nearby were some soldiers from the opposing side. The C.O. ordered the men to come to his aid, to help him get his jeep from the mud.

The goldbricks replied, "Sorry, Sir! We have been declared dead by your forces, and the company observer reported that we were not to contribute any further to the games, Sir!"

"Very well," said the C.O. He turned to his driver. "Private, we need a little traction. Drag some of those dead bodies over here and put 'um under the wheels."

❖❖❖❖❖❖

V

205. Value of Education

Mother Mouse and her three little offspring slowly made their way out of their hole, looking left and right to make sure that the house cat was nowhere in sight. With the coast clear, they marched into the kitchen and began enjoying the crumbs left from the family's latest meal. They were savoring the flavors when from the corner of her eye, Mother Mouse spotted the sneaky approach of the house cat. Since the feline was between them and the safety of the hole, there was only one thing left to do. The mother took a deep breath and bellowed, "Woof! Woof! Woof!"

With a screech of fear, the cat turned tail and bolted from the room. Mother Mouse and the children quickly scurried to the hole for safety. Once they were settled back in the comforts of the hole and had again caught their breath from the excitement, Mother Mouse gathered the little ones for a lesson.

"Now," said Mother Mouse, "do any of you know what lesson we can learn from this experience?"

"No! We don't know, Mother," squeaked the little mice.

"It is this," she said, "It's always good to know a second language!"

✦✦✦✦✦✦

206. Value of One's Spouse

A pastor was sitting in his office when a young man entered asking if the pastor might consider performing the marriage ceremony for him and his wife-to-be. The pastor was glad to oblige, so the two of them began speaking of the arrangements. After several details were discussed, the young man looked embarrassed but finally blurted out a question. "Well, Pastor, how much is your fee for performing this wedding for us?" The pastor responded in his usual manner saying, "Son, there is no set fee; you just give me what you believe she's worth." The young man pulled out $1.00 and handed it to the pastor. Just then, the young man's fiancée entered the office and sat down. The pastor took one look at the bride-to-be, pulled out $1.25 and handed it to the young man and said, "Keep the change, son."

✦✦✦✦✦✦

W

207. Whatever You Think

A young girl's father was very sick, and everywhere she went she asked people to pray for her father. While she was mentioning this prayer request to some friends, a Christian Scientist overheard the need. The lady approached the little girl and quickly reprimanded her saying that indeed her father was not sick! She went on to tell her that sickness is only a matter of the mind and that her father only thought that he was sick.

After a couple of weeks the Christian Scientist saw the little girl walking along the sidewalk downtown. She approached the little girl and asked, "How is your father today?"

"Okay, I guess," she said. "The problem now is that he thinks he's dead!"

◆◆◆◆◆◆

208. What's In a Name?

A group of men who were college buddies got together for a reunion of sorts. Each told the others about his wife . . .

Martin married *Wendy* and his life ever since was a breeze.
John married *Ruby* and got a shimmering jewel.
Bobby married *April* and got showers of blessings.
James married *Rose* and got a fragrant and beautiful flower.
Bill married *Hazel* and got a nut.

◆◆◆◆◆◆

209. When You Grow Up

A pediatrician was almost ready to take some blood from little Johnny; however, Johnny was terrified of the doctor but more so of the needle that was soon to come his way. The doctor approached with the massive-looking syringe in his hand, and Johnny began to cry uncontrollably. This was not the first time the pediatrician had faced such difficulties, so he retreated to a previously successful method of trying to distract the youngster while finishing his detestable deed. The doctor looked pleasantly at Johnny and asked, "Tell me, Johnny, what are you going to do when you grow up?" At that moment, the doctor stuck the needle into Johnny's arm. Johnny screamed out, "I'm going to kill you!"

❖❖❖❖❖❖

210. Which Is Better?

Two goats were rummaging around a Hollywood garbage dump when they came across a tin can with film inside. They kept working until they removed the lid from the top. After stringing out the long film, each goat began consuming the film frame by frame. Once the film was completely eaten, one goat said to the other, "Wow. That was a great film!"

"Yeah," said the other, "but I really thought the book was a lot better."

❖❖❖❖❖❖

211. Which Sermon?

A pastor came to the pulpit at the time for the church's weekly offering. Attempting to encourage a good offering from his congregation, he said, "Folks, today, I have three sermons with me. For an average offering of $100 per family, I have a five-minute sermon. For fifty dollars, I have a fifteen-minute sermon, and my last sermon is a full hour and a half for five dollars. Alright ushers, you come, and we'll see which sermon I should preach."

❖❖❖❖❖❖

212. Which Would You Rather Have?

Dr. Sanderson was asking the students in his English class to ponder which of the great books of literature, apart from the Bible, each would like to have if he or she were stranded on a desert island. Some had said the works of Shakespeare and others various of the great poets. One resourceful student replied, "McAllister's Guide to Practical Shipbuilding."

❖❖❖❖❖❖

213. Who's Crazy?

An old farmer was slowly driving by an insane asylum with his truck loaded down. Along the fence of the facility, an inmate called out to the farmer, "What's in the back of your truck?"

"Manure," replied the farmer.

"What are you going do with it?"

"Put it on my strawberries back at the farm."

The inmate yelled out, "Hah! I might be crazy, but at least I know to put sugar and whipped cream on mine!"

✦✦✦✦✦✦

214. Who's King?

A lion was proudly prancing through the jungle, and he came up to a monkey and asked, "Monkey, who's the king of the jungle?" The monkey replied in a scared tone, "Oh, you are O Lion." Coming up to a zebra, the lion roared, "Zebra, who is the king of the jungle?" "You are, O Lion," he replied. After a short time, the lion approached a giraffe, "Giraffe, who's king of the jungle?" "You are, Mr. Lion," the giraffe quickly acknowledged.

Just then, the lion spotted an elephant. He approached the "mammoth" creature and asked, "Elephant, who is the king of the jungle?" Immediately, the elephant picked up the lion with his trunk and began to bash the lion on the nearest tree.

After throwing him on the ground and pounding him with his mighty feet, the lion feebly stood up with his body bruised, broken, and shaking. He said to the elephant, "Just because you don't know the answer is no reason to get so upset about it!"

✦✦✦✦✦✦

215. Working Day and Night

A man was driving down a country dirt road when suddenly the road became severely muddy. He tried to negotiate the road, but the mud was so deep that his car mired up to the axle. Fortunately, he was able to motion to a nearby farmer to pull his car from the mud with his tractor. The farmer requested five dollars for his services, and the man was glad to pay it. As he did so, he commented to the farmer. "You know, at these prices, I would think that you would do this night and day." The farmer replied, "Can't quite do that. At night I have to cart water to this hole."

✦✦✦✦✦✦

216. Worried About Nothing

During class training for front-line combat, the drill sergeant called Private Jason to the front to answer questions before the entire platoon. The conversation went as follows:

Sergeant: Private. What would you do if you were by yourself, and you were attacked by one thousand foot soldiers from the north?
Private: Sir. I would shoot them all with my rifle, Sir.
Sergeant: What would you do if after that, you saw five hundred soldiers attacking you from the east?
Private: I would shoot them all with my rifle, Sir.
Sergeant: What would you do if after that, you saw seven hundred soldiers attacking you from the west?
Private: I would shoot them all with my rifle, Sir.
Sergeant: (Beginning to yell in anger) Son, what do you mean that you would just shoot them all with your rifle? Tell me, boy, where are you getting all that ammunition?
Private: (Smiling) From the same place you're getting all those soldiers, Sir!

♦♦♦♦♦♦

217. Wrong Destination

A man needed to make a business trip, so he decided to take a train because he could get a little sleep between the destinations. Once arriving on board the New York to Chicago train, he explained to the porter, "Now, I am a heavy sleeper, and I need for you to make sure that I wake up at 3:00 a.m. to get off at Buffalo. I will be hard to get up, and I might resist your efforts; however, at all costs, you must get me off the train at Buffalo."

The next morning, the business man awakened only to realize that the train was pulling in to the Chicago station. Outraged, he found the porter and began upbraiding him unmercifully with harsh and derogatory language. Once the man stormed off the train, another passenger asked the porter, "How could you stand there and so kindly take such verbal abuse from that man?" "Oh, that's nothing," replied the porter, "you should have heard the man I put off at Buffalo!"

♦♦♦♦♦♦

X

218. "X" Marks the Spot

Rick and Jerry rented all the equipment they needed and went out fishing in the middle of the large, county lake. They enjoyed the best luck they every had filling all the coolers with bass. When the day was about complete, they spoke of their desire to return to the same spot for another day of great fishing.

Rick: Why don't we come back tomorrow and fish here some more. I don't believe we'll ever find a better spot than the one we fished today!
Jerry: Sounds great to me. But tell me Rick, how will we ever find this exact spot again?
Rick: Oh come on Jerry! Don't you know anything? I'll show you.

Immediately, Rick began to search through his tackle box. Finally, he came out with a piece of chalk, leaned over the edge, and marked a large "X" on the side of the boat.

Rick: That should do it. "X" marks the spot!
Jerry: Rick, you're crazy! I cannot believe how dumb you are just to put an "X" on the side. How do we know that they'll even rent us the same boat tomorrow?

✦✦✦✦✦✦

Y

219. You First

Four women shoppers got into a horrible argument over some sale items at the local department store. In fact, the disagreement got so horrendous that they began fighting, scraping at one another, pulling hair, and scratching. The sheriff was called to the scene where even he had a difficult time pulling them apart.

Once this was taken care of, they all began to tell their stories at the same time, each trying to out-do the others in her story. Mayhem once again ensued as they yelled and screamed over the sound of the others. The sheriff finally got everyone quieted down again, and using the wisdom of Solomon he declared, "Okay, I will take the time to hear the story of each one of you, but for this to be done calmly and orderly, I will hear the oldest first."

The women looked at each other silently. The case was closed immediately.

✦✦✦✦✦✦

220. You'd Never Believe It

A family had returned home from Sunday school and church, and all were preparing for lunch. As they sat at the table, Mother asked little Johnny, "And what did you learn in Sunday school today?"

He replied, "We learned of how Moses led the Children of Israel out of Egypt."

"Tell us all about it," Mother said.

"Well," said Johnny, "it's like this. Moses was at the front of the whole group when back off in the distance he saw Pharaoh's army coming. There were foot soldiers with M-16's, and tanks were roaring and firing their cannons. Thinking quickly, Moses called in the Navy to make a pontoon bridge across the Red Sea on which the Children of Israel quickly crossed. The bridge was so good that not one Israelite got his foot wet. Anyway, after the Israelites got across the bridge, Pharaoh's army started to cross the bridge too, but Moses radioed for air support. All of sudden, the jets from the Air Force came and bombed the pontoon bridge sending Pharaoh's army into the water and cut off Pharaoh from getting to the Children of Israel."

Mother and Father sat there almost in disbelief. Father said, "Now, Johnny, is that the way your Sunday school teacher told you the story?"

"Well, no," said the little boy, "but if I told you the way she said it happened, you'd never believe it!"

✦✦✦✦✦✦

Z

221.   Zaccheeus, Come Down (a true story)

My niece, when she was almost four years old, had learned many of the Bible stories, and she enjoyed singing the little songs she learned in Sunday school and children's church. While visiting her grandmother and grandfather, she would get up on the fireplace hearth and use it as her stage. On one visit, she was "performing" for her audience and was singing the "Zaccheeus" song. It came out like this:

"Zaccheeus was a wee little man,
And a wee little man was he.
He climbed up in the sycamore tree,
For the Lord he wanted to see.
And as the Savior passed that way,
He looked up in the tree.
And he said, 'Zaccheeus . . .
Come on down! You're the next contestant on the Price is Right!'"

Index

A

advice, 28, 97, 135
ability, 138, 197
absent-minded, 55, 73
abstinence, 64
academics, 48
accommodating, 148
accomplishments, 112
Adam & Eve, 111
admiration, 163
adults, 112
advertising, 33, 81, 83, 92
advice, 171, 172
affection, 86
afraid, 109, 122, 125, 135, 140
afterlife, 36, 73, 154
age, 219
airplane, 58, 61, 122
alcohol, 11, 22
alligators, 129
ancestry, 98
anger, 5, 14, 69, 85, 106, 142, 143, 156, 166, 167, 170, 217, 219
annoyance, 5, 66, 69, 71, 76, 93, 143
answer, 104, 164, 216, 196
anticipation, 152
apology, 124
appearance, 144, 199, 200
application, 143, 157
appreciation, 192
appropriate, 47, 165
approval, 110
argument, 49, 168, 186, 219
arrival, 8, 51, 70

arthritis, 139
assessment, 171, 197
assistance, 118
astonishing, 128, 161
asylum, 13, 97, 133
attacked, 75, 216
attendance, 29, 72, 78, 87, 99
attitude, 21, 41, 66, 67, 76, 85, 137, 161
audition, 119
awakened, 17, 89

B

Bach, 119
bad tasting, 202
bandage, 172
baptism, 195
beauty, 144, 175
bed-time, 25, 141
behavior, 10, 58, 59, 66, 67, 77, 85, 93, 147, 184
belief, 9
bet, 150
better, 142, 165
Bible lesson, 164
bills, 44
blessing, 27, 180
boldness, 197
books, 210, 212
borrowing, 127
bothered, 173
bragging, 105
brainstorm, 33

brat, 10, 58, 85, 93, 100, 106, 135, 198
breakfast, 16, 132
breaking, 127
bribery, 24
bruised, 142, 213
bully, 42
burial, 17, 86
business meeting, 105

C

Cain's wife, 19
calm, 20
calmness, 122, 123
camel, 163
camp, 21
candor, 197
car trouble, 28
care, 191
carried, 201
cat, 57, 101
cement, 106
change, 206
changed life, 11, 21, 22, 67, 136
changes, 203
cheap, 125
chicken 132
children, 106, 112
choice, 159, 210
Christmas, 10, 104
church, 149
clarity, 182
college, 77, 105, 118, 138
colloquialisms, 203
comfort, 45, 158
commands, 159
companionship, 101
company, 101
comparison, 98, 109

competition, 187
complaining, 21, 23, 44, 67, 76, 85, 167
compliment, 59, 113
conference meeting, 180
confession, 175, 190
confident, 109
confusion, 51, 152
consolation, 124, 158, 177
construction, 102
contention, 168
contentment, 191
control, 85, 170
conversion, 136
cooking, 124
correction, 100, 145, 161
correctness, 25, 79, 88
corruption, 24
counseling, 49, 135
country (USA), 181
courage, 6, 42
courtroom, 65
cows, 28, 200
crazy, 208, 213
creation, 144
credit, 201
creditors, 201
cruise, 129
crying, 133, 158, 177
cure, 12, 53, 89, 174, 185, 191
curse, 27
cynical, 130

D

damage, 116
danger, 52
dated, 203
deacon, 3

death, 36, 57, 78, 82, 86, 131, 191, 207
debate, 199
debts, 201
decision, 23, 68, 74, 123, 142, 199, 202
dedication, 132, 137
defeat, 155
definition, 113
dejection, 155
deliverance, 201
denial, 127
departure, 23, 69, 85
depraved, 24, 66
descending, 221
deserted, 212
desire, 77, 90
destination, 217
determination, 19, 63, 74, 90
devastation, 67
devil, 30
devotional, 143
diagnosis, 191, 196
dictator, 31, 69
diet food, 202
diet, 202
difficulty, 121
digression, 38
directions, 2, 32, 57, 69, 74, 79, 86, 92
disappearance, 47
disbelief, 32, 67, 80, 220
discovery, 46
discussion, 9, 55, 74, 77
disdain, 31, 67
disgrace, 131
dishonesty, 116, 176
disobedience, 24, 30, 58, 85, 90, 135, 142, 159, 204
disregard, 35, 69, 71, 80, 85, 93, 171

disruption, 198
distance, 65
distraught, 133
distress, 169
disturbance, 198
diversion, 19, 71
divine will, 34
doctor, 93, 117, 196, 209
documentation, 60
dog, 35, 68, 75, 81, 92, 119, 128, 188
domination, 27, 69, 72
donation, 108
dreams, 125
driving, 103
duel, 42
dust, 36
dynamite, 46

E

eating, 37, 64, 66, 150, 202, 210
editorials, 186
education, 205
effectiveness, 20, 78, 87
effigy, 31
elderly care, 7, 64
elderly, 73, 82, 126
electrocution, 131
elephant, 114, 213
embarrassment, 131, 145, 194
end of the world, 24
enemies, 126
engagement, 1
English, 25, 84, 104, 162, 193
enough, 38, 70, 91
entrance, 72
equality, 86
escape, 179
evangelist, 171
exaggeration, 188, 220
examination, 185

example, 7, 48
excitement, 68, 180
excuses, 19, 71, 74, 80, 136
execution, 131
exercise, 49
expensive treatment, 12
expression of love, 16

F

failure, 61
fairness, 42, 43
faith, 9
failing, 8, 18, 47, 52
falsehood, 176
farewells, 4, 78
farm, 147
fate, 177
fault finding, 127, 128
faults, 190
fear, 12, 18, 109, 122, 125, 129, 135, 140, 205, 209, 213
fed up, 23, 58
feelings 57
fellowship, 45
fertilizer, 213
fiancée, 206
fighting, 14, 15, 42, 49, 75, 91, 142, 186, 213, 216, 219
film, 210
finding a church, 45
finesse, 134
firing squad, 131
fishing, 46, 182, 218
foolish, 50, 165
football, 34
for sale, 188
forceful, 63
foreign language, 205
forfeiture, 169

forgetful, 2, 50, 51, 55, 73
fortune, 52
foul language, 145
foul, 174
freezing 145
friendly, 60
friends, 126
frog, 82
frugality, 56
frustration, 44, 51, 140, 201
full of bologna, 170
fund raising, 33, 44, 211
funeral, 35, 78

G

gambling, 26, 56
gassing, 131
gentleness, 57, 166
getting a crowd, 78
getting worse, 29
gift, 10
giraffe, 213
giving, 11, 137, 211
glutenous, 170
goat, 210
going out, 62, 183
goldbricks, 204
golf, 43, 156
good deeds, 63
gossip, 134, 190
government, 17, 160
grades, 104
grammar, 25, 84
growing up, 209
guessing, 13
guidance, 2
guillotine, 131

H

handouts, 160
hanging, 131
happiness, 4, 40, 67, 68
hard life, 27, 64
hardworking, 20
harshness, 78
hastiness, 69, 134, 185, 192
headlines, 187
heaven, 32, 107
help, 18, 34, 75, 91, 115, 122, 123, 215
henpecked, 72
heredity, 16
history, 24, 98
holding hands, 39
Hollywood, 210
honesty, 59, 184
honor, 161
hopefulness, 152
hopeless, 123
Horrify, 152
humbled, 155
hurried, 99
husbands, 110
hypocrisy, 184

I

ignorance, 28, 32, 80, 81, 84, 88, 105, 146, 167, 193, 213
ignoring, 194
illogical, 160
imagination, 13, 83, 88, 175, 220
imitation, 82
impossibility, 83
impressed, 16, 78, 92
in-laws, 111
inappropriateness, 157
indigestion, 124
indignation, 166
inexperience, 159
inheritance, 82
injured, 172
injustice, 114
innocent, 130
innovation, 88
inquisitive, 144, 145, 163, 183, 196, 213
insanity, 13, 89, 133
insomnia, 12, 89
inspiration, 38, 39
inspirational, 180
instruction, 5, 25, 72, 84, 86, 92, 140, 155
insurance, 116
introduction, 70
intruder, 166
invention, 83
irritation, 40, 69, 71, 76, 89
issues, 160

J

jail, 102, 136
judge, 136
judgement, 7, 91, 103, 136, 176
jumping, 140
justice, 136

K

kindness, 63, 100, 166, 217
king, 213
kissing, 174
knocked out, 14
knowledge, 79, 104, 121, 193
knowledgeable, 146, 182

L

language, 154
late, 63, 99
lawyer, 192
laziness, 69
leaving, 159
leftovers, 21
lesson, 3, 100, 205
lion, 213
listening, 71, 101
literature, 104, 212
logic, 102, 127, 129, 150, 160, 193, 213, 218
loneliness, 107, 121
long life, 126
long-winded, 172, 173, 211
loss, 26, 133, 192
lost, 61, 81, 121, 123
love, 39, 86, 106, 133
luck, 26
lying, 107, 115, 176, 188, 190

M

manliness, 109
manners, 59, 85
marriage, 27, 49, 72, 77, 86, 110, 111, 133, 153, 157, 183, 206
martial arts, 14
mayhem, 58
meanings 113
meanness, 14, 58, 66, 85, 93
measurement, 86
mellow, 113
memorization, 115, 162, 195
memory, 51, 114, 115
message, 211
methods, 46
metric system, 204
miracle, 128
mischievousness, 169
misdeed, 130
mis-diagnosed, 117
misfortune, 26, 52, 57, 80, 116
misquote, 115
mistaken, 75, 117, 138, 163, 185, 194, 207, 218
mistreatment, 188
misunderstanding, 54, 103, 110, 117, 120, 130, 138, 164, 167, 175, 185, 189, 193, 194, 195, 207, 213, 218, 221
mixed up, 115
model, 111
money, 35, 44, 71, 80, 82, 118, 125, 137, 149, 150, 157, 165, 206, 215
monkey, 213
moonshiners, 22
motivation, 18, 78, 204
mouse, 109
moving, 2
mule, 67
music, 119

N

nakedness, 194
name calling, 108, 120
names, 120, 208
needles, 209
needs, 118
nerves, 58
nervous, 8, 19, 97, 122, 195
New Years, 104
newlywed, 124

news, 187
nightmare, 125
not at fault, 127
note-worthy, 187
notes, 152
notification, 17, 81
novelty, 151
numbers, 26

O

obedience, 30, 59, 72, 90, 117, 135, 142, 148, 151, 159, 161, 204
obituary, 131
obligation, 17, 44, 63
offense, 37, 76
offensive, 146
offering, 132, 137, 211
old age, 64
on a roll, 26
once in a life time, 60
opinion, 54, 87, 113, 146
opportunity, 23, 91, 139
optimism, 33, 41, 77, 140
oration, 199
order, 102, 198
orders, 159
out doing, 29, 43, 79, 165, 168, 169, 219
outlook, 41, 74
overboard, 129
overspending, 118, 160

P

paradise, 111
parakeet, 145
parking, 198
pastor, 108, 116, 141

pastoral care, 141
patience, 142
patient, 117
payment, 192, 201
peace, 53, 126
performance, 221
perjury, 197
permission, 110
persistence, 6, 63, 79, 143
perspective, 27, 64, 74, 75, 76, 82, 84, 85, 87, 144, 152, 163, 164
perverse, 145
pessimism, 41, 67, 76, 140
piano, 119
pigs, 66, 132, 146, 147
plan, 215
plenty, 149
point of view, 27, 64, 74, 75, 76, 84, 85, 87
police, 91
politeness, 100, 148
position, 98
positive thinking, 207
postage, 31
potential, 48
powerless, 155
practical, 212
practice, 43, 56, 150, 195
praise, 151
prayer, 6, 34, 36, 66, 99, 154, 180
preacher, 152, 155, 190
preaching, 8, 37, 87, 97
preparation, 153, 154
prepared, 216
preplanning, 215
prescription, 64
pretense, 184
pride, 31, 76, 98, 125, 135, 138, 155, 175, 197

prison, 97, 102, 136
procedure, 102
profanity, 156
professor, 25, 55, 104
profit, 157
promises, 74
proposal, 1, 29, 77
protection, 15, 91, 129, 166
protest, 160
protocol, 159
prunes, 161
psychiatrist, 12, 89, 135
punishment, 90, 145, 161
pushed, 99
puzzle, 138
puzzled, 3, 82

Q

Quaker, 166
qualifications, 92
quality time, 183
quarante, 167
questions, 55, 104, 164, 196, 216
quick thinking, 134, 205
quiet, 53

R

rain, 87, 130
reading, 193, 212
reality, 39, 82
reassurance, 122
receiving, 149
recovery, 4
refinement, 100
reflection, 144
reformation, 11
regroup, 33, 83

relationships, 109, 111, 120, 124, 125, 133, 141, 162, 191, 208
relief, 45
religion, 67
reluctance, 140
remedy, 49
remembering, 218
reminiscing, 153
remuneration, 35, 69, 192, 206, 215
reorganize, 33, 83
repayment, 157
repentance, 200
repetition, 162, 171
reprimand, 108, 207
rescue, 123
resignation, 158
resistance, 30, 63, 71
respect, 39, 163
responsibility, 15, 44, 63
rest, 53
restlessness, 12, 89, 90
restoring, 127
resurrection, 4
retort, 146, 199, 216
retribution, 7, 91, 176
retrieve, 128
rerun, 157, 127
reunion, 208
revenge, 14, 93, 114, 165, 169, 186
revival, 22, 37, 67, 70, 87
reward, 59
riddle, 164
ridicule, 11, 66, 85
risk, 83
rivalry, 43
robbery, 91, 136, 166
romance, 1
Rudolph, 168

S

sacrifice, 132
sadness, 155, 158
safety, 83
sales, 41, 84, 128
salesman, 189
satisfaction, 40
saved, 11
saying the wrong thing, 151
scared, 125, 135, 140, 200, 213
school, 48, 85, 105
Scripture, 143
searching, 169
second language, 205
second opinion, 196
secretive, 13, 50
security, 153
seeking, 169
self control, 170
self-centered, 137
selfish, 137
sensationalism, 187
sentence, 136
sermon, 37, 87, 171, 172, 173, 174, 211
setup 215
sharing ideas, 9, 51
sharing 149
shock, 28, 78
shots, 209
shoved, 99
show, 116
sickness, 76, 124, 141, 207
signs, 169
silence, 1, 23, 93, 156
sin, 175, 176
sinfulness, 107
singing, 113, 221
sleep, 3, 53, 89, 174, 217
small, 47

smell, 174
smelling, 174
snakes, 129
soldiers, 14
solution, 49, 74, 122, 123, 219
songs, 21, 22
spanking, 135
speaking, 97, 100, 101
speech, 100, 101
spiritual presence, 180
spirituality, 132
squirrel, 164
standing up, 3, 15
state of affairs, 24, 181
stature, 47
stealing, 130, 186, 190
story telling, 220
stranded, 212
strength, 6, 18, 56
stubborn, 135, 141, 143
stuck, 215
study, 48, 154
success secret, 20, 56, 78, 126, 182, 183
successful, 18, 92, 138, 182
sufficiency, 216
Sunday school, 54, 103, 112, 115, 137, 149, 220
supervision, 30, 69, 88
supply, 216
support (financial), 118
surprise, 56, 101, 161, 184
surrender, 91
suspicion, 130
swimming, 30
sympathy, 76

T

tact, 134
talent, 119
talkative, 1, 40, 46, 134, 188
talking to God, 154
teacher, 120
teaching, 5, 55
teens, 21
telemarketing, 189
telephone, 5, 71
temperamental, 119
temptation, 30, 175
tension, 168
terminal, 191
testifying, 11, 19, 65, 79
testimony, 139, 180, 197, 220
tests, 104
text selection, 47
thankfulness, 105, 192, 151
theft, 130, 136, 166
therapy, 101
thinking, 207
thirsty, 90
time, 93
timeliness, 61, 99
togetherness, 62
tongue-tied, 195
tornado, 62
toughness, 148
training, 150
trap, 6
trapped, 18
travel, 62
treatment, 185
truth, 197
truthfulness, 8, 65, 79, 82, 107, 190, 194
turn about, 7, 35, 91, 104, 108, 165, 186, 199
turtle, 114

two-faced, 199

U

ugly, 200
umbrella, 130
unavoidable, 189
uncomfortable, 58
understanding, 40, 170, 193, 196
unprovoked reaction, 14
unsuccessful, 18, 83, 140, 155, 156, 189
updating, 203
upset, 133, 213
useless, 7, 83, 204

V

value 125, 206
values, 161
vision, 65
visiting, 147, 148
vocabulary, 162
voice, 113
volunteering, 59
voting, 3
vows, 23

W

walking on water, 128
war games, 204
watching, 143
water, 128, 129
weakness, 60
weather, 168
weeping, 133, 158, 177
weights & measurements, 203
welfare, 160

widowed, 153, 177
widows, 29, 86
will power, 64
willingness, 60
wisdom, 219
witnesses, 116
witnessing, 19, 65, 139
wives, 208
work ethic, 112
work, 84, 92, 112, 167, 215
writing, 24, 118

Z

Zaccheeus, 221
zealous, 139
zebra, 213

Made in the USA
Middletown, DE
03 February 2022